"Bazil Meade didn't invent gosp[...]
and transformed our parents' [...]
public expression of the spiritua[...]
This book tells both his own story and that of a wider, historic movement."

– Trevor Phillips, OBE, Chairman of the Equality and Human Rights Commission

"It has been an enormous pleasure to work with Bazil over the years. He is truly an inspirational man who stops people in their tracks with his extraordinary voice along with the beautiful choir that he has built up. His ability, flair, commitment and passion are inimitable, touching everyone who comes into his path. This book chronicling his amazing journey was long overdue. Readers will derive huge pleasure from his memories and stories."

– Sally Green, owner of Ronnie Scott's

"After decades at the sharp end of Gospel music Bazil Meade turns out to be the Peter Pan of the Gospel scene. His boyhood dream still spawns young talents and keeps them dancing in the aisles."

– Joel Edwards, Director of Micah Challenge

"I'm blessed to have met and worked with Bazil on a number of occasions. Over the years and across the globe, he has reached out to thousands, young and old, with his music and professionalism. This autobiography will be an inspiration to many."

– Rudolph Walker OBE, actor

"It has been an honour and always a great pleasure to perform on many occasions with Bazil and LCGC. It is a humbling and enlightening experience to be amongst people of such wonderful and uplifting talent."

– Paul Carrack, musician

"Nobody has contributed more to Gospel music in Britain over the past thirty years than Bazil Meade. But, even more than that, Bazil had the vision to cross denominational boundaries and create a great community choir for London. Ever since, wherever they have travelled throughout the world, LCGC have been a remarkable unifying example."

– Viv Broughton, owner of the Premises recording and rehearsal studios

A BOY, A JOURNEY, A DREAM

THE STORY OF BAZIL MEADE AND THE LONDON COMMUNITY GOSPEL CHOIR

BAZIL MEADE

AND JAN GREENOUGH

MONARCH
BOOKS
Oxford, UK, & Grand Rapids, Michigan, USA

First published in the UK in 2011 by Monarch Books
(a publishing imprint of Lion Hudson plc)
Wilkinson House, Jordan Hill Road, Oxford OX2 8DR, England
Tel: +44 (0)1865 302750 Fax: +44 (0)1865 302757
Email: monarch@lionhudson.com
www.lionhudson.com

ISBN 978 1 85424 998 2 (print)
ISBN 978 0 85721 211 5 (epub)
ISBN 978 0 85721 210 8 (Kindle)
ISBN 978 0 85721 212 2 (PDF)

Distributed by:
UK: Marston Book Services, PO Box 269, Abingdon, Oxon, OX14 4YN
USA: Kregel Publications, PO Box 2607, Grand Rapids, Michigan 49501

The text paper used in this book has been made from wood
independently certified as having come from sustainable forests.

British Library Cataloguing Data
A catalogue record for this book is available from the British Library.

Printed and bound in the UK by Clays Ltd, St Ives plc.

I dedicate this book to:

All those singers, musicians and crew who have passed through the London Community Gospel Choir since its inception and helped it to become a household name.

My mother, Cyntilya Meade, my father, Fenton Kirwan, and my mentor and surrogate mother, Dr Olive Parris, all of whom have passed on, but whose hands and wise counsel guided and shaped me.

Andrea Encinas, and my children Marlon, Vernetta, Leonn, Stephanie and Ce'anna, who together have made this journey with me and helped the boy to realize his dream.

And finally I give thanks to my Heavenly Father through whom all things are possible.

Contents

Foreword

Bazil Meade was born and raised on the island of Montserrat – my favourite place in the Caribbean. He has lived here in England for most of his life and his dedication to music and singing is second to none. His story is an intriguing one, tracing his life from his childhood to the present day. At an early age he found he had a gift from God – the ability to communicate and inspire people to sing well, and his direction of choirs is brilliant and unique. His music and his faith are to him the most important things that anyone can have. I know the feeling.

He loves his native land and so do I.

Sir George Martin
June 2011

Acknowledgments

I would like to acknowledge first of all my parents, Cyntilya Meade and Fenton Kirwan (who are no longer with me), for the start in life they gave me. I believe my father bred the work ethic in me, saying, "By the sweat of your brow you will eat." He taught me to give 110 per cent effort in providing for my family. My mum gave me her entrepreneurial spirit: she never let her lack of schooling stop her, and it was her hard work and sacrifice that brought me to Britain.

Olive Parris, my mentor from my teenage years onwards, became a surrogate mother to me, and helped me through the most difficult times of my young adult life. She helped me to discover my self-esteem, my faith in God and the gift of music that was latent in me.

I thank Andrea Encinas for the years of her life she gave me, and for giving me our three amazing children. We now share seven beautiful grandchildren. It was her energy and creativity that helped shape LCGC's unique personality and public image.

I must make a special mention of all my children. I'm sorry about all the birthdays and special occasions I missed because I was away working with the choir. My heart was always present with you all, and my ambition to leave a legacy for you has always been my driving force.

Special thanks go to Yvonne White for her support and loyalty to my vision. I don't know if I will ever be able to reward you but I know that you see your efforts as your gift of worship to God, and I thank you for that.

To all the choir members, singers, musicians and others who have joined us over the years: I hope this first effort to chronicle a small part of my story and that of LCGC will give you a sense of pride. You have all been part of this wonderful organization and have helped to build what has become a household name throughout the UK, Europe and the world. Many of the chapter titles in this book are taken from the songs written for the choir, which reflect aspects of our story.

A special thank you goes to Jenny LaTouche for her help in compiling some of the material for this book.

CHAPTER 1

Island in the sun

Bright colours. When I think back to my childhood in Montserrat, it's the colours I remember most: blue sea, deep green forests, pearly blue-grey dawns and red and gold sunsets. As we ran barefoot round the village, played with our friends or swam in the sea, we had no idea we were living in a tropical paradise – it was just home.

The first house I can remember was in Tuitts village, where I lived with my mother's family on a smallholding. We all worked the land, growing our own sweet potatoes, peas and pumpkins to eat, and occasionally enough to sell on and make a little extra money. Like most of the houses on the island, ours had three rooms built of unpainted wood, and stood on four concrete blocks. On Montserrat, if you moved house, you literally did just that: you borrowed a tractor and got some friends to help you lift the whole house off its base and manhandle it onto the back of a trailer, and you drove away and put it down in its new location. The roof was either thatched with grass tied in bunches and laid in overlapping rows, or (if you had the money), covered with corrugated galvanized iron. My father's house had a metal roof, which wasn't so good for keeping the place cool, but better for keeping out the rain. It was wonderful to go to sleep there to the noise of the rain drumming on the roof – I always felt dry, warm and secure.

Our house faced the sea, so as soon as you walked out of the door you could see the deep blue Caribbean, and the beach with its grey and black sand – Montserrat is a volcanic island. The house belonged to my tall, dark, pipe-smoking grandmother. We called her Ma, but her given name was Joana Richards, and she was of Dominican descent. My mum's name was Cyntilya Meade (shortened to Cynti), and my sister, who was six or seven years older than me, was Doreen. In Montserrat there was a strong feeling that people's names should be appropriate and somehow "fit" them, so we were often called by a short form or by one or two nicknames. My brother Errol, who was born with ginger hair (a product of our mixed West African and Iberian genes), was often called Cox. I was christened Leonard Duncan Meade, but I was generally known as Charlie. Bazil was just another pet name which my mum sometimes called me, and I started using it professionally when I was in my twenties.

Montserrat is a small island, ten miles long and seven miles wide, and in my day, before the catastrophic eruption of the Soufrière Hills volcano, it was rich, fertile, and dotted with small villages like ours. The island was discovered by Columbus, taken over by the English just over a century later, and colonized initially by Irish immigrants. That Irish heritage is important: Montserrat's national emblem is the shamrock, and the island's flag and crest show a woman, the figure of Erin of Ireland, complete with her harp. Like most of the West Indies, Montserrat became a centre for the import of African slaves, who worked the plantations of sugar and cotton and produced valuable rum for export. When the slave trade was abolished in the nineteenth century, and sugar prices fell at the same time, most of the plantations became unworkable. The Montserrat Company sold off parcels of land to the local inhabitants, so by my childhood in the 1950s, most of the island was owned by smallholders like my family. The government also leased land to local people like my father to grow cotton.

The history of slavery isn't something Montserratians dwell on, but it perhaps explains one factor of Caribbean life – the ease with which families divide and reform. In the days of slavery, anyone could be bought and sold at any time, no matter what families they had established. When couples were separated, they just had to cope with it, and when they were transferred to another owner and another plantation they would make new relationships. It didn't stop them loving their children – but it was often out of their control whether they stayed with them. It was a pattern that became deeply ingrained.

So although my parents were separated, there was no big scandal attached, as there might have been in England at the same period. After my mum left my dad she had another brief relationship, which produced another boy, Eric, who lived with his father. I lived with my mother, grandmother and Doreen (who had a different father), and my brother Errol stayed with my father. From time to time Dad and Errol would walk over to Tuitts to see us, and it was generally a friendly arrangement.

Montserrat is a British overseas territory: our culture and education were based on the British model, and during the Second World War, men from the West Indies had fought in the British army. So when Britain found itself with a post-war labour shortage, it invited people from our islands to take up the vacant jobs and make a new life in the UK. The first wave of emigrants had left on the *Empire Windrush* in 1948, a ship that stopped in Jamaica to pick up returning servicemen after their leave, and many adventurous young men decided to set off to see the mother country. Since then it had become a routine event. Most families had members who had left for England to find work, and who regularly sent money home to help support their family or to pay for their relatives to come and join them.

In 1958 my mum was one of those who answered the invitation. It was a brave thing for her to do: she couldn't read or write (some Montserratian parents couldn't afford to send their children to school, and kept them at home to work in the fields) and she had no skills. But she believed that she could get a job in England and send money home to help Ma, and in time she planned to bring her children over to join her. So she packed her few belongings in a tiny case and went off to Plymouth, Montserrat's capital, to join the ship that would take her to England.

By this time one of her sisters had moved back to share the little house with Ma and Doreen, and the family decided that since I was now four years old, it was time for me to go back to live with my dad. I imagine they thought that it would be better for me to be with Dad and Errol instead of growing up in a house full of women. I don't remember it as a big change in my life. I already knew my dad because he visited regularly, and I didn't really miss my mum. She was usually working in the fields all day, and I probably spent more time with Ma while Doreen was at school.

My dad's house was in Farms village, a couple of miles away, and it was much the same as Ma's. We had three rooms: a dining/living room, a bedroom for Dad, and another one I shared with Errol. The kitchen, where we cooked on an open fire over wood or coal, was in a separate outbuilding to reduce the risk of the house catching fire. From our front door you looked out through the coconut palms onto Farms Beach, but the big advantage for me was that we were closer to the airport, and I could watch the aircraft coming in to land.

My dad's name was Fenton Kirwan, and I soon learned that he was a well-known character in the village, famous for his hasty temper as much as his hard work. He didn't suffer fools gladly, and when people mimicked his stammer he would make a great show of chasing them off, furiously waving his fists – only partly as a joke. It was risky to take the mickey out of him, and anyone who did so was surely putting their health at risk.

Dad had a straight nose and small features (I think there may have been some Indian element in his ancestry) and he was the fittest bloke in the village, and one of the hardest working. He was generous, and would share or lend whatever he had, but he was fiercely proud of his ability to provide for his family. He worked his own smallholding and looked after his livestock, he leased some cotton fields from the government, and if there was any other government work available (which paid hard cash), he would apply to do that too. What he hated most was laziness, and if either Errol or I showed any sign of it, he made sure we had a rapid wake-up call in the form of a quick smack. If we didn't do our chores as we'd been asked, we knew we'd be punished.

Errol was two years older than me, so he was in charge of caring for the animals, mostly goats and sheep. To begin with I trailed around behind him, carrying water or buckets of feed and doing what he told me. I couldn't have been much help. Once, in the early days, I was loosing a sheep from its tether when it took off, running madly across the field. I didn't dare to let go in case it escaped, so I hung on for dear life as it dragged me behind it, bumping over the uneven ground. Eventually the dead weight of a solidly built four-year-old boy slowed it down, and Errol came panting up to rescue me. I was badly bruised, and my dad was so concerned that he got a friend to take me to the hospital to be checked over.

Dad had land holdings in various places around the village. On the vegetable patch by the house we grew peas, pumpkins and cucumbers. Then there were a couple of fields where the sheep and pigs lived, and on the higher ground up the side of the mountain we grew yams, bananas, dasheens (a root vegetable shaped rather like a parsnip), eddoes (a smaller variety, more like a potato) and cassava (another root vegetable, rich in carbohydrates), which was our staple diet. He was a good cook, and most of our food was tasty and hot, using peppers and nutmeg and other locally grown spices. In the right season we picked cashew nuts and guavas from the trees round about, and we grew "bush tea" (any beverage prepared from locally grown dried leaves) and drank it flavoured with nutmeg and milk. There was always fish to be caught in the river or the sea, and Dad would cook whatever we brought home, whether it was cuttlefish, lobster, conger eel or freshwater shrimp – which the Jamaicans call "janga" but we in Montserrat call "jacktumpy".

Errol and I were good at catching river fish, holding our breath and swimming down to the rocky river bed. You had to lift a rock with one hand and grab with the other – OK if it was a handful of shrimp, but the lobsters were trickier. Their powerful claws could draw blood if they gave you a good nip. Sometimes we pulled too hard, and came up with nothing but the claw in our hand. Our river attracted people from other villages who came there to fish, especially on Good Friday, which was traditionally a "fish-eating" day. We used to make a few extra pennies by selling our catch to those who didn't want the bother of catching their own.

Farms village lay in a valley between the mountains, with a dry river on one side and a full one on the other. From the main road you crossed a bridge and came around the hillside and down a slight slope, and the village opened up to you. I learned my way around by following Errol, running barefoot up the hills and picking our way over the stones in the dried-up river bed. The houses had no running water, but there was a big concrete water tank in the centre of the village, fed by a pipeline from the top of the hill. It was the duty of all the youngsters to fetch water before and after school, and we would congregate there with our galvanized buckets and water pots, taking turns to draw water from one of the taps.

Most families had three or four children, and they would all be assigned duties as soon as they could follow instructions. You understood that as you grew up you had a responsibility to service the household. The parents would be working hard in the fields all day and they expected their children to help as soon as they got home from school. You learned your skills – cooking, growing plants, or tending animals – from watching your parents.

Once I turned five, I started school, and then I had the same routine as Errol. We got up at about 5 a.m., and our first job was to tend the animals in the field by the house, moving them to a new pasture, taking them water or walking them down to the river to drink. Then we would gather some wood for cooking, and bathe and clean up before breakfast, which was usually fruit and bread and cheese, and a cup of bush tea. Sometimes we had "pap", a kind of porridge made with flour, milk and sugar.

All our friends went to Bethel School, which served four villages – Tuitts, Farms, Bramble and Trants. There were six classes, two each for infants, juniors and seniors, but all of us – around 120 kids – worked in one large room. Later on, I remember, a single divider was built, but you still had to concentrate hard on what you were doing, and not be distracted by the class next door doing something different.

The school rules were strict, especially about hygiene. You were expected to come to school looking tidy (only the infants wore their own clothes, everyone else wore uniform), with your face washed, your hair combed, your teeth brushed and your fingernails clean. Teacher Eddy was our headmaster, and he was the one who punished you if you didn't come up to his high standards. I remember getting the strap on one or two occasions, for lateness or for fighting. Teacher Eddy would call you out in front of the whole school and give you two or three whacks with a belt. It left big weals across your back, and you had to sleep on your front for a couple of days. It made you take those rules seriously.

At mid-morning break we had school milk, just as kids did in England, only in our case it was powdered milk made up with water. At lunch time we used to go down to the local bread shop and buy a penny loaf and some lemonade (sugar water with lime juice in it).

School finished at about 2.30 or 3.00 p.m., and on the way home we would stop and check on the animals again. Later on we would help Dad prepare dinner, but unless we had homework, or Dad had extra jobs for us, we could go and play. We met our friends down by the water tank in the village square, where everyone gathered to gossip and socialize.

We didn't see much cash in our village, so we never had "bought" toys, but made our own. A favourite was spinning tops. We carved a smooth pear-shape from some wood and hammered a nail into the bottom. Then we wrapped some string around the top, fastening the other end to a cross-piece of wood to give a firm grip. One top would be placed on the ground for the others to aim at, and then the boys would each spin their own top and throw it at the "sacrifice" top and try to break it. We always sought out the hardest wood to make our tops, in the hope of having the champion.

We didn't have much in the way of tools, either, but we used what we could find. There was always plenty of wood, so we would chop what we needed with a cutlass, then we would use shards of glass or anything else sharp to carve the shape we wanted. Some of the boys were really skilled at making amazing shapes. If you cut bamboo before it became hard, you could easily make a flute, and get a few notes out of it, but that was the nearest I ever got to making music. Dad had a radio and we listened to that, but no one played any instruments in our village. My most exciting Christmas was the year my mum sent me a harmonica from England, but I don't remember being very good at playing it!

We were very poor, but we were never aware of it. In our house there was very little that was manufactured, but we knew that we could always get by as long as we were prepared to work for what we wanted. If you wanted toys, you made them. We were never hungry – provided you were willing to go fishing, or to climb a coconut tree, or to hunt along the beach for the salty sea-grapes that grew there, you could always find something to eat. I suppose that bred in us an understanding of hard work.

Still, we were always keen to make a few extra pennies, and I sometimes used to see the other boys selling charcoal in the village, and talking about their "coal pits", so I pestered Errol to show me how to do it. The best wood for making charcoal grew on the Kusha trees, but they were covered in sharp thorns which got into your hands and feet, which made gathering our supplies a painful business. Even when we were young we each had our own cutlass – we soon learned to be careful with sharp blades – so we used that to cut our wood. Then we dug a rectangular pit and laid the dry wood in the bottom, criss-crossing it and dropping straw into the spaces. We covered the wood with green leaves and then covered the whole thing with dirt, leaving a hole for air. Then we lit the dry grass at the bottom, made sure it was burning and left it to smoulder. After a couple of days we went back and uncovered the pit and picked out the charcoal. We could sell it around the village because charcoal burns much hotter than wood, and people preferred it for cooking.

The extra money was useful for necessities like sugar, matches and kerosene for lamps, as well as treats like sweets and special food we couldn't catch or grow ourselves. You could buy all those things from Tata, who ran the village shop from his living room. Sometimes we bought sea fish from Hogan the fisherman, who took his boat out to sea and sold his catch on the beach. When one of the big boats from Plymouth landed a good catch, the fishermen would load it onto a truck and drive round the island, announcing their arrival in each village by blowing a conch shell like a trumpet. Everything was always bought fresh, because no one had a fridge.

Our village was its own little community, and everyone lived in much the same way. There was only one white man, who lived about two miles outside the village, in a smart, well-kept house surrounded by lots of land. His name was Mr Griffiths, and he was probably descended from one of the big plantation owners, because his family owned the whole estate. I suppose a century earlier he would have owned us all as his slaves. He never came into the village, and I only ever saw him once or twice, from a distance.

I had once seen some white men when Dad took us to Plymouth, but that was all. The closest I came to white folk was Teacher Viyola, who lived in Farms village and was mixed race. Although she taught us in school, she didn't mix with the rest of the village much, and lived differently: there were books and a piano in her house. She had a daughter, but Hilary didn't play with the rest of us. She had very light brown skin, and that set her socially on a higher plane altogether.

When we saw our teachers in the street, we always addressed them respectfully, as "Teacher Viyola" or "Teacher Ellis". Children never addressed adults by their first name – that would earn you a slap, and if you went home and told your parent why someone had slapped you, you would get another. It was a very disciplined society. Years later, when I visited Ghana as an adult, I was surprised to see exactly the same conventions there; there was a code of expected behaviour, and the children understood it. If they spoke to an adult they always used their title, and if the person was a stranger, they would address them as "Mister", or even "Uncle" or "Auntie", just as we used to.

On Sundays we always went to church with Dad, wearing our best church clothes. The main denominations all had churches on the island, and most of them had missions. The big churches (like the Methodist church next door to the school) were more formal, and attracted people with a bit more money. The missions were more lowly places, which accepted you as you were. Dad had been brought up a Methodist, but we went to the Pentecostal mission. It didn't have an organ or other accompaniment to the singing – just voices and a tambourine. Errol and I found it quite boring, but we had to go.

Just about everyone on the island was nominally Christian, but that didn't stop people being very superstitious. Everyone believed in ghosts, and there were lots of incidents where people claimed they had seen the dead walking. Perhaps that general acceptance made us more ready to believe that we saw things, too.

Every year in early summer, when the mango season came round, we would go and check the trees for ripe mangoes – it was a case of the early bird getting the first fruit. One of the biggest mango trees was clearly visible from the edge of the village, and Errol and I kept an eye on the fruit. When it looked almost ready to drop, we laid our plans. We went to bed early so as to be sure to wake up in good time, and set off in the dusk before the dawn. Off the main road there was a path leading to the dry river bed, and it was lined with mango trees. As we made our way down it, we grew more and more disappointed – our greedy eyes had deceived us, and there were hardly any ripe mangoes lying on the ground.

The moon was still up, and the path was gloomy; the shadows between the trees were even darker, and we began to feel nervous. Every rustle in the undergrowth made us jump. Then Errol looked back along the path and thought he saw two people coming towards us.

"Look!" he hissed, pulling me back into the bushes. "Jumbies!"

My hair stood on end. Jumbies are spirits of the dead, and in the old obeah beliefs of the West Indies (a mix of Anglican doctrine with traditional African folklore), jumbies could travel around and possess people. I shivered. We were only about three minutes from home, but there was no way we were going to pass those two shadowy shapes. We hesitated for a moment or two, then without another word, we both took to our heels and ran away, down to the river bed, across the stones and all round the edge of the village the long way round, till we got home.

We might have forgotten all about it, but a while later something similar happened. We were playing in the square when we heard screams, and a girl came running down the path from the river, shouting that a man was after her. We looked up and saw a figure in the distance, disappearing into the undergrowth. She said that she had been looking for mangoes on the path when she realized someone was following her – a man who had died earlier that year. Even then, Errol and I never told our friends about our own experience. We didn't want them saying we were scared.

The most exciting time of year was Christmas, and our preparations began when we killed the pig. Most people bought a suckling pig in the summer and reared it all year, because Christmas dinner was always succulent roast pork. But most importantly, it was the time of the December Festival, which is to Montserrat what Carnival is to the rest of the West Indies. Throughout the month, masquerade troupes would move from village to village, collecting money. They were an amazing sight: they wore tall headdresses and masks, and vivid costumes of striped or patchwork tunics covered with streamers, ribbons, bells and mirrors.

As soon as we heard the distinctive sound of the fife, triangle and goatskin drums, we would all rush down to the square to watch. The dancers (usually a group of men and young boys) were led by a maestro, cracking his whip on the ground like a ringmaster to keep the crowds back, or perhaps to drive evil spirits away. He was the most confident of all, striding around the group and leading them from house to house, and picking up the money people threw at their feet. We would watch spellbound as the dancers performed, their streamers flying as they made their complicated stepping movements, to a rhythmic and repetitive tune on the fife. Sometimes they were accompanied by a Moko Jumbie, a masked man on stilts.

The December Festival is thought to have started as a plantation tradition, when the slaves were given a three-day holiday. Certainly it has a flavour of Africa about it, with the drumming and the dancing, though the fife and some of the heel-and-toe polka steps may reflect the Irish elements of the island's history. The Moko Jumbie, too, is thought to have been part of African folk religion – a tall, strong spirit-man who could protect people from demons. When their native beliefs were suppressed by the slave owners, the people kept them alive in their traditional dances.

Masquerade is one of my few musical memories from Montserrat; probably its rhythms run deep at the roots of my musical awareness, and underlie some of my music even today.

Once the masquerade troupes had gone, we had the excitement of our Christmas parcels. Within the island there wasn't much to buy or give as gifts, but those who had emigrated sent parcels home for the family two or three times a year, and the best were always the Christmas parcels. Dad would get a message from the post office in Plymouth to go and collect them. They mostly contained practical things, like clothes and shoes, but that was exciting because we didn't have much of either. We wore shorts and tee-shirts all year round, with a similar uniform for school, and a clean version for church on Sunday. New shirts or light jackets were very special. I had never owned a pair of shoes until my mother sent me some from England, and I was so proud of them. The other big treat was the candy – which was always seaside rock. We spent most of Christmas sucking away with our cheeks bulging!

My mother always kept in touch, though it must have been hard for her. She still couldn't read or write, and she had to find someone to write letters for her and address the parcels. She would tell Dad what she was doing, and where she was working, and how she was always trying to get the money together to send for us. I don't remember her describing England much, so I just imagined it to be an island like our own.

Eventually, she sent for Doreen first. The money arrived in a registered letter, and Ma packed Doreen's things and took her to Plymouth to join the boat. I'd only been to Plymouth once, and it was so big and bustling and exciting, and it seemed to be such a long journey, that I felt as if I had visited a foreign country. I was more envious of Doreen seeing the big city than of her adventure to Britain. I knew that one day it would be my turn, but it didn't bother me. Many of my friends had already made the journey: one day they'd be sitting next to you in school, and the next they had disappeared, and you never saw them again. It was a fact of life on Montserrat, and probably throughout the British West Indies in those days.

I was nine when the letter came. It was an ordinary school day just before Christmas, and Errol and I came racing each other up the path to the house. Errol was winning, but he stopped when he saw Dad standing in the doorway with an envelope in his hand.

"Charlie," Dad said to me, "Yu Mada sen fi yu."

I stood absolutely still for a minute, not knowing what to say.

Then Errol punched my arm. "Yu goin' to Englan', Charlie!"

CHAPTER 2

Long long lonely journey

By the time I got to school the next day I had told all my friends the news, so it wasn't a surprise to them when Teacher Eddy made the formal announcement in assembly: "Charlie is leaving us for England." He made similar statements several times a term, as various families sent for their children to join them. It wasn't just children who left: new emigrants were always saving money and planning their move, too. There was a Governor General on every British island who passed on government promotions about subsidized fares and the ready availability of jobs, enticing thousands of West Indians to make the journey. The rest of us never stopped to wonder what kind of lives our friends were going to. We knew Great Britain was an island, too, and we just supposed that the mother-country would be much like our home. Maybe a bit bigger.

Christmas that year passed in a blur. There was so much to do, and it involved a couple of trips into Plymouth for a passport and to buy clothes. I was more excited about that than about the prospect of going to England. For a start, we got to travel by bus.

The driver was a man called Rapa who owned a truck. He had fitted wooden benches in the back, and drove it round the island on the main roads, stopping at the junctions where smaller paths led to the villages. People would wait there and climb on, clutching their shopping bags or the boxes of goods they intended to sell in

Plymouth – mainly meat or vegetables for the market. It was noisy and crowded, and very uncomfortable as the truck bounced and swerved along the roads.

Plymouth seemed like a metropolis to me – a huge place full of shops and offices and traffic, with smartly dressed workers hurrying along the streets, so different from the slower pace of life in our village. Dad bought me new shirts and shorts, but there were no warm clothes to be found: why would anyone need a woolly jumper in our tropical climate? I needed things to travel with – my own towel and wash bag – but we also bought gifts for me to take to Mum. Expatriate Montserratians had a long list of the things they missed from home, and those travelling to England were commissioned to carry their requests, like bottles of Bay Rum and a green cologne called Limacol. The average suitcase arriving in England with an immigrant would have mystified any Customs and Excise officer who happened to examine it: a bare minimum of clothes and belongings, but layers of brown-paper packages containing mangoes, guavas, bush tea, and packets of tree bark, leaves and seeds to make the folk medicines that we generally relied on.

I didn't have time to worry or brood about my future, and it wasn't in my nine-year-old nature to do so. I was a little sad about leaving my friends and Errol, but going to England seemed to be programmed into us as something both desirable and inevitable. Everyone spoke of it as a good thing, a better life, and anyway, when your dad told you something was going to happen, you just got on with it. So when the day of my departure came, I felt excited but not worried. There were two other young men from our village going on the same boat, so we all travelled to Plymouth together in a car. I was squeezed in the back seat with them, while Dad travelled in the front next to the driver.

This time we drove right through the middle of the town and down to the docks where the ships berthed. When I played on the beach near my house I had often seen ships passing in the distance, on their way to or from Plymouth, but of course they were far away. Now I saw one up close, I couldn't believe how enormous it was – like a whole street of the huge Plymouth buildings floating on the water. All around us on the dock people were saying their farewells. Dad handed me my little brown valise.

"Charlie, yu be a good bwoy, now. Don' be no trouble to Gilbert here."

I nodded and looked up at Gilbert and his brother John. Dad had asked them to look after me, so they were my guardians for the duration of the trip. The Spanish-registered immigrant ship, *SS Begona*, was one of three ships running this route between Britain and the West Indies, and the crew were experienced in dealing with people leaving their homes for the first time. They always put people from the same villages together in the shared cabins, so I'd be seeing a lot of these two guys over the next five weeks.

"Don' worry, Bouloo," said Gilbert, using Dad's nickname. "We keep an eye on yu bwoy." He shook hands with Dad, put one hand on my shoulder and steered me towards the gangway. It seemed very steep. I gripped my suitcase in one hand and reached out with the other to grasp the rope running up the side, but just then the whole walkway shuddered – it must have been Gilbert stamping his heavy feet behind me – and I almost fell. Gilbert spared a hand to steady me, and turned to flash a grin at Dad. Falling in the sea would not have been a good start to my journey.

I was glad to get onto the deck – at least it was level – and I turned to look down. Dad looked somehow small standing below me on the dock. I gave him a quick wave goodbye, then I was hustled through an iron door and down lots of metal staircases to find our cabin. The big square room had eight bunks in it, and Gilbert told me to put my case on one of the bottom bunks, because he didn't trust me to climb up and down safely. He showed me where the bathroom was, with its flushing toilet and porcelain sinks and shiny taps, and as we came out we felt the whole ship begin to vibrate and shudder as the engines started.

It took me a while to find my way back up through the maze of staircases to the upper decks again. By the time I reached the open air we were out at sea, and Plymouth, with its busy streets and white buildings, was already receding into the distance. I squinted into the glare, but I couldn't pick out the dock, or Dad standing there. I took a deep breath of the sea air, but it was full of the chemical smell of diesel, and made me want to cough. I stood for a while looking out over the rail, until I became aware that I felt slightly dizzy. The boat was beginning to roll gently, and I realized that the blue sea which looked so flat from the beach was actually a series of waves. I decided that what I really needed was the bathroom again.

I was sick for several days. I don't think it was sea-sickness alone, but a combination of that and nerves, a reaction to the shock of leaving home on my own. I stayed in my bunk, close to that useful bathroom, and tried to shut out the unfamiliar sounds and smells of the old boat.

The worst thing was the cooking. On the few occasions in those early days when I made my way down to the dining room, my stomach would heave at the pervasive smell of stale cooking oil. At home we had our main meal in the evening, and I was used to a small breakfast and less lunch. Here there were three huge meals a day, and the food was unfamiliar: the standard British meat and two veg, with what we would call Irish potatoes (different from the sweet potatoes of home), boiled, mashed or fried, often with tinned peas. It all tasted very bland and heavy compared with the spicy, fresh food I was used to.

There was one day when my seasickness was at its height. The sea was particularly rough, and every time I lifted my head from my pillow the dreadful nausea would overwhelm me. All I could do was lie as still as possible, and I felt as if the voyage would never end. Tears trickled onto my pillow: I was ill and alone and completely miserable. Gilbert and John were off around the ship all day, enjoying their holiday. It was an adventure for them, meeting people from other islands, eyeing up the young women, and socializing in the dining room and on the decks. As long as I was safely in my bunk each evening, they didn't worry about me too much.

Eventually, after a couple of weeks, I began to feel better. I got used to the motion of the ship, and at last I was able to keep my food down. I got up and began to venture around the boat, going up on deck to feel the sun on my face and breathe the sea air, keeping upwind of the diesel-smelling engines. I was fascinated by the gulls which followed the boat and came swooping low over my head, and wished I had my slingshot with me to bring them down, as I would at home. For a long while I thought these were the birds being served as food, because they looked about the same size as the chicken being dished up for dinner.

Once I had stopped being sick, I began to enjoy myself, and the dreadful lonely feeling began to fade away. Even so, I had very little contact with anyone else: there must have been other children on the boat, but I don't remember meeting any of them. My social circle was the seven adults who shared my cabin, and they didn't have much to say to me. I wasn't worried. My upbringing had made me mature beyond my years, mentally as well as physically; I was a self-contained boy, and stoical about things I couldn't change. I don't remember being particularly introspective, or concerned about what awaited me in England. I just took one day at a time. I found my way around the boat, explored every corridor and stairway, ate large meals I didn't enjoy, watched the people milling around the public areas, and gazed out to sea, looking for other boats and any sight of land.

As the weeks went by I began to notice something odd – the air was cooler, and there were more cloudy days. Sometimes you hardly saw the sun at all, and when you did it seemed paler and weaker than usual. I shivered in my thin shirt and shorts, and was glad to get back to the warm fug of the dining room and the smell of hot food. I had no idea how far north I had travelled. By the time we were approaching our destination, I was spending most of the day inside. It was February, and the decks were uninviting: the sea was the same grey as the sky, with white-topped waves, and a biting wind which dashed icy spray into your face.

On board there was a growing sense of excitement. Most of my fellow travellers were on their way to realize a long-held dream: a life in England, the mother-country. They would be welcomed as children of the Empire, and offered the opportunities they longed for – work, a better quality of life, and the chance to send money home to families who mostly lived in poverty. Most people arrived with a definite plan: they intended to work solidly for five years, earn money and then go back home. A few of them kept an open mind about the future, but the adults mainly had better information than I did about England. They had heard that it was a cold country, where in winter you walked on snow and ice, and for half the year you had to wear two or three layers of clothing. They had no intention of staying there for ever.

I had begun to realize that the weather, at least, was likely to be different from home. I hadn't seen the sun for over a week, and the temperature outside was freezing. But I still had a vague idea that I was going from one small island to another, and of course it would not feel foreign, because we all spoke the same language, we had the same Queen, and everything at home, from the schools to the legal system, was modelled on England. I re-packed my small suitcase eagerly, and went up with Gilbert to watch as the coastline got closer and closer.

The sea had suddenly become much busier: all around us there were boats of all sizes, and tugboats were hooting as they moved about busily. I could see tall buildings on the shore, and cranes and warehouses and cars and hundreds of people. Our ship eased gingerly into its berth, and I gazed down in astonishment at the dockside: all the people were white! I had only ever seen a couple of white faces in my life, apart from the crew of the *Begona*, and now there were all these pale-skinned people walking around, carrying suitcases or pushing luggage carts or heaving on ropes. There were vans and lorries, and all the drivers and the dock staff wore smart uniforms. It was extraordinary.

An announcement came over the intercom: "We are now arriving in Southampton. Please be ready to disembark with your luggage. If you have coats, you should put them on now." Someone understood the English weather, at least. I didn't have a coat, of course, and neither did Gilbert or John, so we stood shivering by the rail as we waited our turn to go down the gangway. At least they wore long trousers: I was still in my shirt and shorts.

Down on the dockside there were suddenly a lot more black faces, as families came to meet their loved ones off the boat. All around us people were shouting and waving, greeting friends and relatives who had come to claim them. Aunties and uncles were exclaiming over how much children had grown, friends were smiling broadly and exchanging handshakes or hugs. Gilbert and John's friends arrived but Gilbert explained that he was responsible for me and they had to wait for my mother. I began to be anxious: would I even recognize her? Would she recognize me? She hadn't seen me since I was four.

Gradually the crowds thinned as people went off in groups, until only a few of us remained. Gilbert turned to me.

"Charlie, I caan keep these folks waitin' no longer. We got to tek yu somewhere to wait."

One of his friends pointed to a building across the way. "Tek him a Laas Property, man. Dey look after him."

So they led me off to the Lost Property Office, where a kindly white man in a smart uniform sat behind a desk. Gilbert explained that I was waiting for my mother, and handed me over with a look of relief. He rubbed my head with a heavy hand. "Yu be OK now, Charlie. Be good," and he was gone – my last link with home.

The man kept talking to me, but he had a strange accent, and although I knew he had to be speaking English, I could hardly understand him. I was cold and tired and shy and intimidated by my surroundings. At least his office was warm. Then I felt in my pocket and my fingers closed around a scrap of paper, which I handed up to him.

"Mrs Cyntilya Meade," he said. "This your mother's name, lad?" I smiled and nodded. At least I understood that. He left me sitting on a hard wooden bench while he went out with my paper.

A few minutes later the door opened again, and my mother came in, along with the official and a strange man.

"Charlie!" My mum enveloped me in a rare hug. "Yu got here!" I understood her relief. She had no way of knowing whether I had even caught the boat. "You cole?" I nodded. "Put this on." Over her arm she had a thick winter coat, which proved to be much too big for me; she turned the sleeves back so I had the use of my hands. Then she produced a blue woolly hat, which she put on my head. It made my scalp itch. She thanked the official and led me out onto the dock.

"Charlie, this here is Joseph. He yu' stepfather. An this –" she indicated another man, standing beside an old Ford Consul, "is Uncle Ben. He drivin' us."

The two men sat in front, and I sat in the back beside Mum, with my face pressed against the window. The longest drive I had ever made until then was the forty-minute drive from Farms village to Plymouth. The journey from Southampton to London seemed to go on for ever, and it was through the strangest landscape I had ever seen. I was used to open spaces, fields and forests and beaches, and scattered small settlements where the houses were all built of wood. In Plymouth I had seen cobbled streets, and some brick-built houses and offices, but the town retained an old-fashioned, scruffy air from its piratical past. The houses there had wooden hurricane shutters, and people generally didn't bother with glass in the windows.

Now I was driving along metalled roads edged with solid pavements, and more houses and huge buildings made of brick and stone than I had ever seen in my life. (It was a long time before I managed to get my head around the idea that in England, a thatched house was seen as desirable and classy. In Montserrat it just meant you were poor.) It took an age to get out of Southampton, along roads full of cars and buses. Then we drove through what I could recognize as countryside, though there were no leaves on the trees and the hedges looked dry and brown and dead. It was raining. I dozed.

When I opened my eyes we were in South London, and I was astonished all over again. In the tropics darkness falls quickly: it is dusk at 5 p.m. and pitch dark by 6, and we had one electric light in the middle of the village square. Here in England the dull grey afternoon was giving way to a seemingly endless twilight. As the darkness gathered slowly, lights went on in the houses on both sides of the road, and there were street-lamps, too, every few yards. All the shops had huge, brightly lit windows. I had never seen so many lights.

The pavements were still full of pedestrians – more people than I had ever seen – but these were not the brightly dressed crowds you would see in the Caribbean. These people were huddled under umbrellas and muffled up with hats and scarves, and their winter coats were all dark brown, black or navy blue. It all looked very gloomy.

Our house was in Thistlethwaite Road, Lower Clapton: a terrace house with bay windows and five steps up to the front door. It was owned by Mr and Mrs Morgan, who lived on the ground floor with their two children; there was another family in the basement; we lived on the first floor, with another man, Freddo, in the room behind ours; and there was someone else in the attic above us. We had one room, with a box room next door where my sister Doreen slept. I didn't recognize Doreen. She was sixteen now, practically grown up, and she spoke with an English accent and dressed like an English teenager. What surprised me even more was that she had a tiny baby in her arms: my new sister Roselyn. Mum hadn't mentioned that she and Joseph had just had a baby.

I suppose it was quite a crowded house. The neighbours were always changing, as people arrived, found work and moved on. My stepfather and my mother slept in the big front room with Roselyn, and I had a mattress on their floor. There was a paraffin stove in the room, too – in theory we shared the kitchen, but the house-owners had a prior claim on it, and rather than wait for them, Mum preferred to cook on the stove in our room. She was out at work during the day, so Doreen and I would start preparing the evening meal when we got home from school, and Mum would cook it when she got in.

During the day, Roselyn went to a childminder (another Montserratian) while Mum worked in the local paper factory. Mr Levy's labour force was mostly composed of immigrants, and most of them developed problems with their hearing: the noise levels in the factory were too high for anyone to conduct a conversation, and in those days before Health and Safety regulations there was no protection from the damage. Mum became quite deaf in later life.

Over the next few weeks my dazed feeling wore off, and I gradually became accustomed to my new life in cold, grey England. Mum bought me airmail letters so I could write home to Dad and Errol, folding up the flimsy blue paper and licking the glued flaps round three sides to seal it. Sometimes I put a note into the registered letters Mum sent to Dad when she was enclosing money. I tried to describe what England was like, but mostly I asked questions about what Errol was doing, and how my favourite animals were. When I imagined them opening my letter, standing in their own little house with the door open to the sun and the sea, it seemed like a different world.

As I settled in, I began to understand more about England. Young though I was, I saw that life wasn't easy for immigrants. We were lucky to have somewhere to live, even though it was only two rooms. I saw signs in other lodging-house windows which said "No Irish, No Blacks, No dogs." Doreen took me shopping with her and I became aware of a level of hostility wherever we went. In cafés people would move away from your table: you never felt welcome. There still were not that many black people around in London in the early sixties, and you were always walking on eggshells. People driving past you in the street would open their car windows and shout abuse: "Go back where you came from!" was the least of it.

I realized later that much of this hostility was based on ignorance. Most English people had no idea where Montserrat was; they often thought we had come from Africa. They did not realize that our islands were British colonies, and that West Indians had fought and died in the British army and air force during the war. Very few of them understood that we were there at the invitation of the government, who needed people to fill vacant jobs in crucial areas like transport, hospitals and factories. As I grew familiar with the dynamics of the different cultures, I realized that most English people knew only what they had seen and heard about black people in films, and their attitudes were conditioned by scenes of rural Africa rather than the West Indies. They thought we were uneducated natives. When the evacuation of Montserrat brought an influx of children into British schools, their teachers were surprised to find them generally ahead of English children of the same age: West Indian schools were founded on the English system but were more highly disciplined and rather traditional in their teaching methods.

Once I had settled in, my mother registered me at the local school, Millfields Primary. I was nervous on my first day, walking into a playground full of white children. There was only one other black boy in the school, but fortunately he was in my class and took me under his wing. Georgie had been in England since he was a baby, so he spoke perfect English (people still sometimes didn't understand my accent). He was also the most fluent reader in the school, and he was always the one picked to read in assembly. My family knew his – nearly all the local immigrant families were acquainted with each other – so they were happy that we were friends. Sometimes I went to Georgie's house after school; like me, he was expected to help around the house, but I was surprised when he got out a frying pan and made us a plate of chips for an after-school snack.

I got into trouble on my first day at school. The boys were all hanging around together in the playground, playing a game called "Bundle". It was a typical boys' scuffle, where they barged around and knocked each other down. There was one boy who seemed to be doing a lot of the pushing, but for some reason no one was touching him. I joined in the fun, and chose that boy to push. He turned round and punched me in the face – definitely not part of the game! That was like a red rag to a bull – maybe I had a little of my dad's temper in me. I jumped on him and grabbed his jacket, and we rolled on the floor together. I was much stronger than him – years of working in the fields had built up my muscles – and I was definitely getting the better of the fight when a teacher strode over and separated us. We were both taken inside and reprimanded, and I was glad this school was not in the village back on Montserrat. There our parents would have heard about it and would have given us another telling off, but here there was no reason for Mum to find out.

There was a positive side to that incident. The boy I hit was the school bully – which was why no one else dared touch him. Once the other boys had seen him crying in the playground, he lost all his aura of power, and he never bullied anyone in that school again. Meanwhile, taking him on, albeit by accident, had given me a reputation for courage and strength, so I never had any trouble from anyone else.

Having a friend like Georgie helped me a lot, too. He was established and accepted, and had friends among the white boys and girls. I was treated rather differently, as much because I was the new boy as because I was black. There was a certain amount of name-calling and abuse, but Georgie was very sensible and just ignored it, so I did the same.

In spite of the fact that the other kids seemed to think that black skin meant you were dirty, I was shocked at how grimy some of those inner-city children were. At home we had no running water, but we bathed in the river every day, and always went to school with combed hair and clean nails. Some of these kids didn't even own a toothbrush, and most of them never had a bath. In our house there was only one bathroom for fourteen people, but Mum made sure that we washed in a basin of hot water every day, heating a kettle on the paraffin stove.

"No reason you caan be clean, Charlie," she said, "jus' cos it too cole to go in de river."

You wouldn't want to bathe in the river in London, anyway, I thought. On the few occasions I saw it, the Thames looked as though you would come out dirtier than you went in.

It soon became clear that I wasn't cut out to be academic, but Teacher Eddy's school had prepared me well, and I certainly wasn't behind the others in my studies. I just found studying dull. Where I did excel was at sports. Again, my physical strength was an advantage: I was not taller, but I was definitely better built (and probably better nourished) than most of my class. And I had some skills already: on Montserrat we played a lot of cricket. Admittedly, we didn't have much of a pitch – just an uneven field or the beach – but then, in London we played on a tarmac playground. At home, the bat was a branch off a coconut tree, and the ball was a lime or a young breadfruit, or almost anything round that could take a battering. But it got my eye in, and with my strong arms I could whack the ball right out to the boundary (the brick walls around the playground) almost every time.

Later on, when we moved to a house in nearby Stamford Hill, I moved to a new school where they really appreciated my talent for cricket. Our team was in the East London Primary School finals, and in one day I made seventy-four runs and took six wickets. They called me "The Black Bomber", and I was definitely the man of the match! It gave me a lot of confidence to know that I could represent the school and do well.

We moved house several times, because my mother and stepfather were always trying to find somewhere a little bit better, with a bit more space. We stayed in areas where there were other West Indians, because not many white people would accept us as tenants. The immigrants kept together, welcoming in newcomers and helping them to find jobs and lodgings. People tended to keep with their own kind, and stay where they felt at home.

It was the same with church. West Indian immigrants were facing all the problems of settling into a culture which they expected to be familiar, but which turned out to be alien in so many ways; they also found that their reception among ordinary English people was not only unwelcoming but often actively hostile, and so they turned for comfort to the church. Sadly there, too, they were received with indifference at best. In addition, they often found the English style of worship restrained and formal, so many of them responded by starting their own congregations, renting church halls and community centres to begin with, and later pooling their resources to buy their own premises. Often these black-led churches were Pentecostal in nature, emphasizing the importance of the Holy Spirit in enabling Christians to live faithful lives. They also tended to attract people from the same parts of the West Indies: within their communities you would find that people stayed with others from the same island. So Jamaicans had churches with Jamaican pastors, and Bajans[1] had churches with Bajan pastors. Sometimes a whole church would be made up of people from one small district of an island. Our church had a congregation of around a hundred, who met in a hall behind some shops; the Montserratian pastor and his family lived in a flat above.

Mum was very strict about going to church and wearing your Sunday best, but I thought it was boring. We had church in the morning, and then afternoon Sunday School as well. At first I went along with a good grace, but once we had bought our first television, I really resented having to leave the Sunday afternoon Western to go out to Sunday School. At ten or eleven years old, I had no idea how important church would be to me one day.

CHAPTER 3

Found myself a reason

My mother and stepfather worked hard. They were always trying to get together enough money to provide a better life for the family, and get us better living conditions. Like most immigrant families, we moved around from one rented flat to another, but every time we managed to get a bit more living space, the family seemed to increase. Those two rooms in Thistlethwaite Road would have been fine for Mum, Joseph and Doreen – but then baby Roselyn arrived and so did I.

My stepfather, Joseph Greenaway, came from Montserrat, too, but from the north side of the island, about two miles away from us. In Montserrat terms, that made him practically a foreigner. He worked at the Watneys brewery in Whitechapel, leaving home at seven in the morning and returning around seven at night – later if he managed to get some overtime. That meant that I really only saw him for an hour or so before I went to bed, and we got on OK. He let me try some of the Mackeson stout he brought home from work, and laughed when he saw how much I liked the strong, bitter taste.

Doreen was kind to me, too, though a bit distant: she didn't really want to have a kid brother around. Her interests were those of any teenage girl – clothes and pop music and boys and her school friends. At least I had known I would be living with Doreen. The real surprise to me was Roselyn, who was born in February, a couple of weeks before I landed in Southampton. Living in our all-male household in Farms, I'd never had anything to do with babies before. Now I was up close to a screaming, demanding, sometimes smelly baby, who would be dumped in my arms if Mum and Doreen were busy with other things. I learned to jiggle her up and down and stop her crying, how to make up a bottle and feed her, and even how to change nappies. Those were the days before disposables, with terry nappies which had to be sluiced off in the toilet, then put in a nappy bucket filled with water and bleach, and later washed. At least Mum did that part, but I often managed the nappy changing, folding the heavy material into a triangle and carefully fixing it with a safety pin.

While Roselyn was very young she woke a couple of times in the night to be fed. Mum would put on the light and step over my mattress on the floor to make up a bottle of milk, then go back to bed and feed her. I just turned over, pulled the blanket over my head and went back to sleep. I was used to sleeping with light and background noise: my mother and stepfather were still up and usually listening to the radio when I went to bed. I got used to it like everything else, and when Roselyn started to smile at me, I began to enjoy playing with her and rocking her off to sleep.

The real surprise to me was how much time I had to spend indoors. In Montserrat I was always outside, whenever I wasn't in school or in bed. I only stayed in when it was raining (and not always then). Here it was often too cold to play outside, and there was nowhere to go except the street, anyway. No hills to run up, no river to fish, no trees to climb, no sea to swim in. Even the chores I had to do at home – fetching water, tending the animals, picking cotton or weeding the vegetables – were all outside jobs. Here my life was very different.

When I got home from school I had to help Doreen start the dinner. Mum would leave the food out before she went to work, and we would peel the vegetables and get the stove going, so she could finish the cooking when she got in. We couldn't get much Caribbean food in London in those days, only a few spices dried and ground in packets. We were used to eating lamb and goat, but Mum could make a good stew with neck of lamb or mutton, with English vegetables in it. When other West Indian families arrived, they would bring herbs and spices with them – peppers, whole nutmeg, pimientos and fresh thyme.

At school I enjoyed the school dinners, and my tastes were very different from those of my English friends. Most of them disliked vegetables, so I used to help them clear their plates of cabbage and carrots and broccoli. I liked the school meat pie, and always went back for second helpings, but I hated the greasy chips that everyone else loved. I was used to a healthy diet: Dad had taught me to drink the broth that greens were cooked in, because the goodness was in the water.

Mum used to get home about six o'clock, having picked up Roselyn from the childminder on her way. One of us looked after the baby while she cooked, and we ate at about seven thirty when my stepfather got in.

What with cooking and homework and baby-minding, I didn't have a lot of time to myself. We didn't have a television when I first arrived in England, but we did have a radiogram, a substantial piece of furniture made of highly polished wood, with a radio in the top and a gramophone underneath. Mum liked to listen to *The Archers*, but I liked playing our collection of records. Most West Indian families had a stack of records by Jim Reeves, because he had a repertoire of religious songs, but I liked Cliff Richard, the Beatles, Otis Redding and Sam Cooke, too. We had Bluebeat records, with ska and reggae – styles from Jamaica, which has been supplying the world with music for a long time.

Mum also tried to encourage me to do some reading. Although she couldn't read herself (none of her siblings went to school), she believed fervently in the importance of education for her children, and she wanted us to get on in the world. Unfortunately I wasn't a great reader. We were ploughing through *Gulliver's Travels* at school, but even though the hero went to such strange and fantastical places, I couldn't get interested in it. I found the style of writing hard work to read. What I really loved were my comics, which I bought from the newsagent on the corner of the street – all the superheroes like Superman and Batman, and the more mundane *Beano* and *Dandy*.

After a year or so we moved house again, this time to Cazenove Road, Stoke Newington, not very far away. In the late 1950s and early 1960s, this was a predominantly Jewish area, and many of the houses were rented in multiple lets to immigrant families. Conditions were not good; these were the days when Rachmanism[2] was rife, and unscrupulous landlords would buy up slum properties and fill them with immigrants who had little choice of where to live, because of the effective (though unofficial) colour bar that was in operation.

Families like ours were desperate for somewhere to live, and usually unaware of any legal rights they might have as tenants. Often the houses were very dilapidated, and repairs were seldom done, although the rents were always collected on time. There were frequent arguments between the tenants, with complaints that children made too much noise, or that music was played too loudly, or that people were leaving the shared facilities dirty. Some of the families were of African origin rather than West Indian – a distinction the English were unaware of, seeing only black skin, but which caused yet more problems. Their culture and food were different again, and the smells of unfamiliar foods lingered on the stairs and landings, causing yet more bad feeling.

Doreen had left school and moved out to live independently, so our two bedrooms in the new house should have been ample for the four of us. However, Mum had scraped together some more money, and this time she sent for Eric, her son who had lived with his father in Montserrat for the last nine years. My cousin Gwendolyn was also sent over by her family, and Mum said she could live with us, too. So we divided the bigger room in half with a curtain, and Eric and Roselyn and I slept in one half, with my parents in the other. Gwendolyn, as a teenage girl, took Doreen's place in the second little room. I suppose it was a bit claustrophobic. Most of the rooms in the house were inhabited by four or more people. The couple next door had two children, and when I got older I used to babysit for them sometimes – I still see those kids, grown up now, around east London.

The arrival of my half-brother Eric was no surprise to me – the pattern of constantly shifting, informal adult relationships, producing various children, was part of the Caribbean culture. Having several half-sisters and half-brothers was a common family structure, and the fact that the adults seldom bothered with marriage didn't prevent them from creating strong family ties, with complex networks of responsibilities and interdependence. This belief in the strength of the extended family meant that the transatlantic traffic was two-way: people often sent their teenagers back to the Caribbean to learn about their culture at first hand, fearing that this strong family feeling would be lost in their attempts to become assimilated in the UK.

In particular, there was always concern about young black boys growing up in what was perceived to be the liberal British environment. It was thought that some time living in a tightly knit family in the home country would teach them respect and discipline. It was a major struggle for West Indian families, who wanted to perpetuate the manners and lifestyle of their homeland. There was friction as children were exposed to the behaviour of their classmates at school, and picked up what were thought to be disrespectful habits. Our increasingly British mindset came into conflict with our parents' Caribbean attitudes, and they were shocked to hear us "talking back" or failing to acknowledge adult acquaintances with a formal "Good morning, Mr Smith." Punishment always followed promptly if word got back to them that we were guilty of this.

When I was eleven I transferred from primary school to Brook House Comprehensive, a school of 1,300 boys. I didn't have an auspicious start. My parents didn't understand the system, and I suppose that even if a letter arrived, my mother couldn't have read it, so they didn't realize that they were supposed to put my name down on a list somewhere. It wasn't until a few days after the start of term that it all got sorted out, and I presented myself at the school – by which time everyone else already seemed to know their way around. To make matters worse, my mother didn't know about the navy-blue school uniform, either, so I started school in a brown jacket and trousers. There was no way I could avoid standing out, a lone black face in the wrong clothes among a class full of white boys.

It was a difficult time for me. The teenagers were not as accepting as the children in my primary school had been, and there was plenty of racist abuse, loud talk about foreigners and immigrants, and plenty of golliwog jokes. There was no escape from it – your black skin is part of who you are, and you can't hide – so I had to make the best of it and learn to stand up for myself. There were only five black boys in the school. One was older than me, but I knew him from Montserrat, and two of the others joined in the same year as me, so we stuck together. Fights in the playground were unavoidable, but I was still strong for my age, so I knew I could hold my own. And I made friends among the white boys who weren't prejudiced, which helped a lot. I soon realized that it was a question of background: the boys who were racist all came from racist homes.

I'd never been particularly academic, but I worked pretty hard. There was lots of homework, and it had to be done – these were the days of corporal punishment in schools, so if your homework wasn't completed, the teachers would use the cane or the slipper as they chose. There would be no complaint from your parents. I can't say that I enjoyed the lessons, but my stoical attitude came to my rescue: I was good at putting up with things.

However, there were compensations. Secondary school was a lot more interesting, with its science and technical departments, metalwork and carpentry. My favourite subjects were English and geography, but algebra was a shock – I'd never been much of a hand at maths. I hated music lessons in particular. All we listened to was classical music, the things the teachers liked, and not anything the kids might like and listen to from choice.

The one thing I excelled in was sport, and now I had the opportunity to take part in a wide range of activities – boxing, cricket, rugby, football and athletics. My early upbringing of physical activity and hard work came to my aid once again. I still wasn't particularly tall for my age, but I was physically strong and athletic. I got on well with all the sports teachers, because theirs was the one class in which I really paid attention, and they were keen to encourage talent. I was soon selected for all the school teams, and sport began to take up most of my time in the evenings and weekends, doing extra practice and travelling to matches. My parents couldn't afford to buy me the proper kit – I played football in plimsolls when everyone else had boots – but sometimes I borrowed the right kit when we were playing away, so I didn't stand out too much.

My teacher was pleased to have a natural cricketer in the team, and later on he arranged for me to go for a trial at Essex County Cricket Club, but my parents turned down the chance. They didn't understand what it meant, and anyway my mum was fixated on the idea that we had to have a good education, and to her that meant book-learning, not hitting balls around. She was convinced that getting some exams was the only way to get a good job and earn some decent money. She knew enough about the gruelling physical labour involved in manual jobs, which paid so little, and money was a constant worry. I always walked the couple of miles to school because there was no cash to spare for bus fares.

At the same time, my parents were becoming a bit irritated by having what they saw as a young adult hanging around the house, writing in exercise books instead of contributing some effort. In Montserrat, even if I was still in school during the day, I would have been working the fields in the evenings and weekends, and having something to show for my work – food we could eat or sell. Here I just did homework, and that didn't help the family. Like any teenage boy, I played football in the playground and scuffed the toes of my shoes and tore the knees of my trousers, or got into fights and ripped the badge off my blazer. Even when I wasn't destroying my clothes I was growing out of them, and it was all more expense.

"Hurry up an' leave school an' get yuself a job," my mum would grumble, looking in her purse to see if she had enough for a new school shirt. I felt that I was just costing them money all the time; even my dinner money was a drain on the family resources. I began to look forward to leaving school and starting work – to stop my parents moaning at me, if nothing else.

Gwen had escaped by getting married, so we were back to two parents and three kids, but even the extra space wasn't enough for Mum. She didn't like the house we were in, so she found us another one in Dalston Lane, about two miles away, on the border between Dalston and Clapton. This house was amazing – a four-bedroom house with a ground-floor annexe inhabited by the owner, an elderly English man. He seemed quite happy to have a black family upstairs (which was itself unusual) and we were delighted to have more space. I wondered briefly whether I was about to have a room of my own for the first time, but life in West Indian families is seldom so simple.

First of all, Mum sent for Errol to come to England. I was excited about this – it was years since I'd seen him, and he had always been my best friend back home. He had shot up so he was a head and shoulders taller than me, but he still had the same wide smile and crazy sense of humour. We picked up where we left off, and it soon seemed as though we'd never been apart. Errol was sixteen now and had left school, so he went out and got a job.

Then we were joined by Joycelyn – she was Joseph's daughter, and she had been living in Birmingham with her mother, but she wanted to come to London, so she joined the family, too, and we were seven in a four-bedroom house. Joycelyn and Roselyn (who was now five years old) shared one room, Eric and I shared another, and Errol had his own room. My mum and stepfather had their own room to themselves at last, but it didn't seem to improve things. We could still hear them arguing.

Their relationship had been deteriorating for a while, mostly (I think) because my stepfather was becoming increasingly irritated with all of us. Everything we did was wrong – if we talked we were making too much noise; if we were quiet we were sullen and rude. No job was done quickly enough or thoroughly enough, and Roselyn was always under his feet with her toys. Even his daughter Joycelyn came in for his abuse, as he ridiculed her clothes, her friends, and everything she did. He banned any of our friends from visiting the house, saying that he didn't want them sitting around in the kitchen, and he wouldn't allow them in the bedrooms as he didn't know what we were up to. We older ones all started spending as much time out of the house as we could, but Eric and little Roselyn didn't have any choice but to stay at home and be picked on. Mum would try to stand up for us, but that only made him turn on her, and tell her what a bad job she'd made of bringing up such greedy, noisy, ungrateful and disrespectful children.

I wonder now whether he had just got tired of our situation, working hard with all these young mouths to feed. Maybe he just felt it was time to move on. But whatever the cause, he was making our lives – and especially Mum's – a misery. I often saw tears in her eyes as my stepfather shouted at her, and it made me angry. I wanted so much to protect her and the younger children, but there was nothing I could do.

Still, it was great having Errol living with us. I was full of admiration for my brother. Here he was, newly arrived from Southampton, in a country where he knew no one, and meeting the mother he hadn't seen for ten years. He should have been overwhelmed, but instead he seemed cheerful and confident. I suppose the difference was that I had arrived as a nine-year-old with a very limited understanding of the world. Errol was sixteen, had finished school, and he had plans. Montserrat bred a maturity and independence in its young men, and Errol knew exactly why he had made the long journey across the Atlantic. He wanted a better quality of life and a job that paid well, and he was ready to go out and find it.

He settled in fast. Within a week he had found a job in a pie factory almost opposite our house, so he didn't have far to travel. He could tumble out of bed in the morning and into his clothes and be at work within five minutes. He found the work easy – operating the machinery that made the pie fillings – and he earned good money. When he brought home his first week's wages, he took out some money for Mum, to pay for his food and rent, and then he went out and bought himself a Spanish guitar. I was spellbound.

He could already play a little – back home he had been hanging around with some friends who liked music, and he had got someone to show him how to play a few chords. He knew enough to play a little calypso, the most popular music in the Caribbean, with its distinctive rhythms and lilting melodies. I hovered behind his chair as he sat in the living room, strumming away and singing. It was like magic, being able to get music out of the instrument like that. I pestered him to show me some chords, too, and I tried to pick out tunes I knew. When I got home from school every day I rushed to get my homework over, so I could spend some time on the guitar before Errol came home from work and reclaimed it.

The only place I'd seen instruments played live was in church, so it came naturally to strum along to the simple choruses we sang there. I would perch awkwardly on the armchair with the guitar on my knee, and sing softly:

By and by,
When the morning comes
When all the saints of God are gathered home
We will tell the story how we overcome
And we'll understand it better by and by.[3]

Church was an important part of my life. School was boring and home was often an uncomfortable place to be, so it was a good thing that there was somewhere else I could go, where I had good friends to spend time with, and where I always felt welcome. It was ironic, I suppose, that as the swinging sixties got under way, and teenage rebellion was in the air, the place where I found my personal freedom was the church.

Church was important to all Montserratian immigrants – it was the place where we gathered among our own people, a little bit of home in England. My stepfather didn't often go to church, but Mum made sure that all the rest of the family did. Our church was The New Testament Church of God on the corner of Cricketfield Road, Clapton, and on Sundays we really did wear our Sunday best. You wouldn't turn up for worship dressed in anything casual. The women all wore smart dresses and hats (in those days no female head was ever seen uncovered in church – if a woman neglected to wear a head covering she would be "preached against", i.e. publicly criticized from the pulpit), and generally looked as though they were going to a wedding. The men were spruced up, too; I had a smart beige suit and my Sunday footwear was a pair of brown pointy-toed shoes, which looked very stylish. It was unfortunate that they were two sizes too small and very uncomfortable, but we couldn't afford new ones – yet another reminder that I wasn't working and bringing in money like Errol. It was unthinkable that I should go to church wearing my everyday shoes (which did fit) instead.

The service was informal and free-flowing, but generally followed the same pattern. If you arrived early at church you would see people kneeling at the altar: the elders and others would be praying for the service before it began. At 10.30 the person appointed for that day would go to the front and lead the "Song Service" – two or three choruses from our hymn book, *Redemption Songs*. These would be accompanied by guitars (the minister and several other people played guitar) and sometimes tambourines. We also had one member who played the piano rather badly, but fortunately she didn't accompany the singing every week.

The songs would be interspersed with prayers from the prayer leader, standing among the congregation, followed by specific prayer requests; people would stand up where they were and ask for prayer, explaining a little about their need. From the Song Service we moved into a time of testimony, when people would talk about what God had done for them. Sometimes they recounted how they became a Christian, or told about something that had happened to them that week, some difficulty overcome or a time when they felt that God was especially close to them. It was intended to encourage and build up your faith, and you couldn't help absorbing the stories and the atmosphere of total reliance on God. These testimonies would also be interspersed with choruses.

There would be the usual church notices – mostly about the church building, I seem to remember. We had recently purchased it, and as it was about 100 years old, it was always in need of repair. There was more singing and then the minister was invited to preach. Our Pastor at that time was R. L. Kennedy, a highly intelligent man who happened to be an electronics expert. He preached very intellectual, analytical sermons, explaining the biblical language and teaching. He knew a lot about Bible history, and I used to get thoroughly lost in his accounts of genealogy in the Old Testament.

Then there was the altar call – an invitation for those who had not yet accepted Christ to ask him into their life – and prayer for those who came forward. Then there was yet more singing, prayers and a final benediction. It was a long morning.

When I was younger I wouldn't be in the service the whole time, of course, but spent most of the morning in Sunday School. Our classes finished early so we could rejoin our parents in church before the main service ended. We got a good grounding in our faith there, listening to stories, singing songs and drawing pictures, and learning a Bible verse which we would be expected to remember for the following week. Our teachers were determined that all the children should be familiar with their Bible and understand it.

When I was about fourteen, though, I started staying in church with Errol. The Pastor had a spare guitar, and he loaned it to me so we could both accompany the singing. I was enthusiastic: I thought it was a great improvement on sitting in the pew. Errol, however, wasn't so keen. He had other things to do with Sunday mornings (like lying in bed, or going out to meet his girlfriend), and since he was older, independent (and earning), Mum wasn't so bothered about making him go to church. She was still in charge of me, though, and I wasn't allowed a choice, so I made the best of it and concentrated on developing my guitar technique.

Up until then I had been playing on Errol's acoustic guitar, picking and strumming. Now I had an electric guitar on loan, and had to develop my skills a bit. To accompany congregational singing I needed to provide both the tune and the background chords, which demanded more skill than I had at the time. Fortunately Pastor Kennedy was keen to help me, and offered to give me lessons on a Saturday morning, so I added that to my sports activities, and managed to be out of the house almost the whole weekend. In view of the difficulties I was having with my stepfather, I felt that this was a good thing.

The Pastor was a great help in my early attempts to learn music, but there was someone much more important to me: the Assistant Pastor, an impressive young lady called Olive Parris. She was of mixed race: her father was Scottish and her mother Jamaican. She herself was born in Jamaica, later moved to Trinidad (where she was a Salvation Army Major) and then came to England, where she began attending a Pentecostal church. She was a gifted musician, playing the piano and guitar, and an inspirational teacher and youth leader.

The New Testament Church of God had a thriving youth community which emerged from its Sunday School. It was great for me to find myself part of such a large group of teenagers of both sexes, and membership of the youth group gave me a strong tie to the church. We bonded into a tightly knit friendship group – we all went to different schools where we were in the minority: odd black faces in classes full of white kids, but here we were all together with a common culture, shared experiences of immigration, and united in a faith that was neither shared nor expressed in the same way in the world outside.

Olive Parris set up singing and drama groups for us, meeting on weekday evenings to rehearse. I joined the singing group, and used the guitar to accompany our choir of about fifteen young people. We prepared performances for the youth conventions within the wider church, which were hugely exciting as they brought together churches from the district or even across the whole country. When we played at the district conventions there would be five or six guitarists from different churches playing together, along with drummers and other musicians. We couldn't wait for Convention time, and the chance to meet friends and make music together, and perform our songs. I was always nervous beforehand – I wanted to perform well – but it gave me a great buzz to be up there on the platform with a large congregation singing along.

All this kept me securely within the church. I got pleasure from the social side of things, meeting people and making friends, and I loved the music. I liked arranging new songs and helping people learn to sing them – it was all very basic compared with what I do now, but it felt wonderful. Music was the magnet that kept me firmly attached to my faith and my church family, at a time when other young people often drifted away.

We had our main youth group meeting on a Tuesday night, and that involved running our own service. It was more relaxed than the formal Sunday worship: the young people led it, reading poems, performing drama sketches and singing. Pastor Parris would preach a mini-sermon, but mainly she simply facilitated something that was offered by young people for other young people. Sometimes we invited others to preach: Joel Edwards (who is about my age) was a member of a sister church in Willesden, and even as a teenager he was a good speaker. He was invited to preach at our youth church.

Olive Parris was also a gifted preacher and teacher. As her name became more widely known, she began to be invited to lead revival meetings for the New Testament churches all over the country. She always sang (as a form of prayer) before preaching her sermon – and she had a lovely voice. It was through playing with her that I learned how to accompany a soloist, how to follow the singer's lead and not dictate the mood and tempo of the music.

Her preaching invitations often meant being away from home for several days, as churches would set up week-long events, and she would take with her a small team of people to help her. They would support her in prayer, and also greet those who came forward at the altar call, pray with them, and offer the laying on of hands for healing. She was immensely popular, and as people heard about her, our church became a very desirable place to worship. As she drew people in, our membership grew and grew, and our youth group increased in numbers too. It all felt wonderfully vibrant and alive, and an exciting place to be.

It was this success which caused a rift in the church. There was so much interest in the revival meetings that Pastor Parris began to produce a small newsletter for those who had attended: it included accounts of what happened at events, and followed up and expanded the message she had delivered. She called it *The Latter Rain Outpouring Revival.*[4]

Unfortunately the leaders of our church took exception to this. They called her before the elders and accused her of starting her own movement within the church. They insisted that she change the title of her little magazine to the name of the church as a whole: *The New Testament Church of God Newsletter.*

I believe the problem was that the hierarchy of the church was uncomfortable with her success, and felt that she should be controlled more firmly by the leaders. All the positions in the upper echelons of the church were held by men, and though women were accepted for certain roles – there was no bar on women preaching, for instance – it was felt that they should always be answerable to a male leadership. They probably felt threatened by her popularity, too. Olive Parris was young, very beautiful and confident. She also had a wonderfully warm way of relating to people, and this was reflected in her success in winning people over and leading them to faith. While the male preachers I heard often relied on preaching allegiance to the church as an organization, Pastor Parris brought people into the kingdom by preaching healing for the soul. While the men emphasized the importance of doctrine, she believed fervently in the importance of people as individuals, and their personal relationship with Christ.

In the end Pastor Parris was told to present herself before a board of elders, which included the overseers of the entire denomination, as well as the leaders of our own individual church. They wanted to bring her revival meetings under their own control, as well as her newsletter. They offered her an ultimatum: she could do as they told her to, or she could leave the church. She chose to leave.

Sadly, this divided the congregation. Our Assistant Pastor had many supporters, and they chose to accompany her when she left the church. Many of those who left were young people – she had a particular gift for relating to youngsters and working with them. My family stayed behind, but I was sixteen now, and growing in independence, and I was devoted to Olive Parris. She had encouraged me in my attempts to develop my guitar playing, and she had also become a listening ear for my youthful troubles. Never judgmental like some adults, she treated young people like friends and equals, while still giving us good advice. I left the church with her. My mother didn't raise any objection, because she was only too glad that I was going to stay within the faith.

Of course, the fledgling church didn't have a building to meet in, but fortunately Pastor Parris's landlord had been a member of our church, and he supported her when she left, and came too. He gave her permission to use the large living room of his house as a place of worship, and that's where the new organization began. It was called by the name of the newsletter: The Latter Rain Outpouring Revival.

My friend Carl Boothe had left the church along with me, and we began to sing duets together. When Olive Parris continued her travels, leading revival meetings around the country, Carl and I went too, as part of the team. It was very exciting to me to be travelling around, outside London, and working alongside the others. Wherever we went, we would be given hospitality by the members of the church we were visiting, so I started meeting all sorts of people from outside our own community. One of our own members was a kind man called Kenneth Dunkley, who owned a white van, and Brother Ken felt that his ministry entailed driving Pastor Parris and the team wherever they had to go. He felt it was a calling from God, that he should provide the transport she needed, and he was pleased to put himself at her service.

Olive Parris was always known as "Mum Parris", and she was like another mother to the young people in her care. She made sure we were taken care of, and that we had a good time, as well as ensuring that our faith was nurtured by the work we were doing. When we were on the road in the van, we'd often sing hymns in harmony, playing the tambourines and guitars in the back. One day we were stopped by a policeman who thought there might be something wrong with the wheel-bearings, because he could hear a rhythmic rattle coming from the van – it was, of course, the sound of an enthusiastically wielded tambourine!

In between trips we held our services and meetings in the house church. By this time I had told Mum Parris a little about conditions at home, and how worried I was by my stepfather's attitude to us kids and to my mother. She knew I was unhappy, and one evening she invited me round to talk about things. There was a piano in the room behind the worship space, and after we had been talking for a while, Mum Parris moved over to the instrument and started playing softly. Music was always a form of prayer to her, and I suspect it helped her to think, and to lift up to God whatever problems she had.

She was thoughtful for a while, and then she looked up and asked me if I could play the piano. I had never tried – our cramped and crowded houses never had room for a piano – but she showed me one or two chords and left me to tinker, while she went out of the room. When she came back she was holding a hymn book, and she started singing. Without thinking I accompanied her, and my fingers found the notes I needed to fit in with the song. In between verses, I found myself improvising on the tune, adding runs and upper parts to embellish the melody. Mum Parris stood watching me in some surprise. She saw something in what I was doing which neither of us had expected – the revelation of a gift.

When I had finished, she put the book down, placed her hands on my head and began to pray:

"O Lord, I ask you to touch this young man and bless his hands. Teach him and lead him. As he plays, let the people who hear him be healed, let them be set free in their hearts and minds. Let him be like David with his harp, casting out devils in your presence, and bringing your Spirit into every act of worship." She prayed for some time; I sat there beneath her hands, listening to her lovely voice prophesying, and gradually her conviction entered into me. The idea took root in me that I was being offered a great gift, and I determined that I would try to be worthy of it. I would learn to play the keyboard, even though I had no idea how I had managed to play the way I had that evening. I would trust God to do his work in me, and use me as he chose.

Before I left that evening I played songs and improvised accompaniments to tunes I hadn't ever heard before. I walked home in a kind of daze, with melodies and rhythms running round and round in my head.

Of course, I didn't have an instrument to practise on, but Mum Parris solved that problem. Until then all her revival meetings had been under the auspices of the New Testament Church of God, but now she was planning her first independent meeting. She went out and bought an electronic keyboard called a Farfisa, and handed it to me. I played it in services for the next two Sundays, but the following week we led a revival meeting in Seven Sisters Road, North London. It was just three weeks since that laying on of hands, and already I was playing in public. It was my first experience of improvisation at the keyboard for a large congregation – somehow I could just hear and feel what to do. I couldn't read music, but I didn't need to; what I played came straight from my spirit.

CHAPTER 4

Constant is his love

I left school when I was sixteen, with no qualifications except basic Maths and English, and no idea what I wanted to do with my life. I only knew that academic work didn't interest me, and I would never achieve anything by staying in the classroom.

I presented myself at the Labour Exchange the week after leaving school, where they gave me the details of a job at a factory in Leyton, East London, machining wood to make furniture parts. The smiling girl who handed over the card wasn't to know that I was to become a regular customer over the next couple of years.

I hated it. I thought I would be learning a trade, but instead I was just moved around the factory, doing menial jobs as I was needed – sweeping the floor or packing parts in boxes. I worked on a massive shop floor filled with machinery so noisy you could hardly think, let alone speak to anyone. I didn't like the rigid routine of clocking in and timed tea breaks, because it felt as though every moment of my time was regimented.

Eventually I got the sack. I was supposedly apprenticed to a man in his thirties, but I wasn't learning anything, and I got fed up with the way he talked to me, shouting orders as if I was his servant. One day I snapped and shouted back at him, refused to do whatever he had asked, told him to stuff his job and walked out.

Back I went to the girl at the Labour Exchange, who this time sent me to a sign-writer. That job didn't last long: I cut my arm on a sheet of metal and had to have stitches. I decided it wasn't for me. The next job I tried was in Spurlings Garage in Shoreditch, where I was supposed to learn to be a car mechanic. It seemed good at first, because I met two other lads from school there, and we could have a laugh together. Unfortunately the job involved day release to the local college, and I had a bit of a block about being sent back to the classroom. The other lads weren't a good influence, either – alone I might have buckled down, but together we tended to talk in class and mess about. Our tutors complained and all three of us were sacked.

This trail of disasters did me no good at all in the critical eyes of my stepfather. He never had a good word to say to me anyway, but he had worked hard all his life, and my repeatedly being out of work infuriated him.

"Yu useless bwoy, yu no good," he used to say. "Yu never gon hol' down a job."

If I answered back or tried to explain what had happened, he would be furious.

"Yu tink yu a man? Yu jus' a bwoy – don' talk back to me."

It wasn't the Caribbean way for children to talk back to adults. I was a teenager, just beginning to grow up, but until I was earning and independent, Joseph would always think of me as a child.

Mum didn't say much, but I knew she was disappointed. I found it depressing, too. What was wrong with me? Joseph, my mother and even Errol worked in factories and didn't seem to mind. They kept the same jobs for years, while I barely lasted three months most of the time. I knew it wasn't because I was lazy, though Joseph accused me of that. Looking back, I can see that I felt dissatisfied with factory work and wanted something more. I disliked being bossed about by someone else, and it seemed to me that in order to keep a job you had to have a subservient state of mind, and be happy to be told what to do every minute of the day.

Like many teenagers, I had a growing sense of a wide world of opportunity outside my door, and I longed to prove myself, to be someone, but the harsh reality of everyday life always beat me down. A lot of the anger I felt was due to the constant attacks on my self-esteem. I felt I was continually being put down not only at home (by my stepfather's verbal abuse), but also at school and now at work. As a boy my skills were sporting rather than academic, but as a black boy I didn't have the same freedom to achieve as the majority of my classmates. In those days immigrants were still a very small minority, and we didn't have the black role models in sport that you see nowadays. No amount of talent and skill would open the doors of opportunity for a black boy as they did for the whites. In the playground and the classroom and the factory it was the same: an atmosphere of mild abuse and preconceived ideas about my low abilities, even from the teachers and bosses.

It's hard to realize just how far the laws against racial abuse have brought us. The first UK Race Relations Act came into force in 1965, forbidding discrimination on the grounds of colour, race, or ethnic or national origins in public places. However, it didn't cover housing or employment, and didn't make racial discrimination a criminal offence. It has taken over forty years to effect a change in mindset so that now it is socially unacceptable (in most circles) to talk about "niggers" or assume that black people are incapable of the same achievements as white people. (There are, of course, always some sections of society which seem to be intractably racist.) In the 1960s you just got used to name-calling in the street, and to the fact that no one expected you to make anything of your life.

The constant friction at home didn't help me. My mother and stepfather always seemed to be arguing. Every so often things would calm down for a while and life at home would be relatively peaceful. But you could never relax with Joseph: he was a volatile character, and he would explode with anger without warning, over the tiniest things, and you never knew who his anger would be aimed at – me or my mum or Errol. In fact, around this time, Errol decided to get married and he left home. I had a room to myself for the first time in my life, but I missed my brother. He was a placid young man, and he was better than me at calming Joseph down. I seemed to enrage him just by living in the house.

Now I was the eldest son, and I felt responsible, particularly for my mum. Her relationship with my stepfather was increasingly fraught, and I couldn't bear to see the depth of her unhappiness. I often heard them arguing, and several times I suspected that Mum's bumps and bruises were caused by him hitting her.

One day in particular I was going upstairs when I heard raised voices coming from their bedroom. The door was ajar and I clearly heard the slap of Joseph's hand round Mum's face. She cried out and at the sound of her wailing something in me snapped. I pushed open the door and shouted at him:

"Leave her alone, man!"

Joseph bent and picked something up off a chair, then turned and pushed me out onto the landing.

"What yu want, lickle bwoy?" he jeered. He raised his hand and I saw he was holding a hammer. I was terrified – I knew he wouldn't hesitate to use it – but I saw myself as the other man in the house, and it was up to me to protect my mother. I stood my ground.

"Yu touch my mum again an I'll fix yu!" I shouted back at him.

It made him even angrier. He pushed me up against the toilet door and thrust his face close to mine.

"Yu shut yu mout', bwoy," he snarled, "or I crack yu skull wi' dis hammer."

I pushed him away from me – I was still strong for my age – and ran off down the stairs.

Joseph was shouting after me, "Only one man live in dis house here – yu get out, bwoy!"

I thought it was time I left home, too.

A few months later I found myself out of work yet again. I knew what Joseph would have to say about it, so I went out of the house at the same time as usual in the morning, though Mum knew I wasn't going to work. To fill the days, I hung around the West End, drifting around the Leicester Square area and hanging out with a group of other unemployed youths. A man approached us and said he was recruiting salesmen to go to Germany – his company sold encyclopaedias, and apparently there was good money to be made selling on the American army bases over there. We would be paid commission only, but we'd get accommodation, and we could earn good money.

This sounded like an adventure, and two days later I and a couple of other young men met at the arranged pick-up point with our suitcases packed, and were driven overnight to Germany. Mum had been pleased that I'd got a job again, and she didn't question whether her seventeen-year-old son could manage alone in a country where he didn't speak the language. She knew I was sensible and resourceful.

Of course, it turned out badly. Our employer hadn't made the arrangements he promised, and the accommodation turned out to be the hallway of someone's house. We did get a lift out to the army base, but we weren't allowed in all the areas, and although we knocked on doors for a week, we didn't sell a single book.

I soon realized I'd been "had" – there was no easy money to be made, and I was paying for my food and sleeping on the floor. I felt a bit like the prodigal son,[5] only I'd missed out on the good times and fast living. I was going to have to swallow my pride and make my way back to England. At least there I could speak the language, and had a chance of getting another job. The other boys stayed on: they were still hopeful that they could start selling soon, but I decided to cut my losses. I went to the station and got a train to France, made my way to Calais (all without speaking any French or German) and took a ferry back to England. At Dover I bought a train ticket to London, and then sat and thought about what lay ahead.

All my hopes for adventure had been dashed. Instead of coming home triumphantly with cash in my pocket, I had nothing. The attack by my stepfather was still fresh in my mind, and I never wanted to see him again. I used the last of my money to make a phone call to Olive Parris. I told her that I was on my way, but that I didn't want to go back home. She understood instantly.

"Come here, Bazil," she said. "We've got a spare bedroom. You can stay here."

This started a new phase in my life. I didn't realize it then, but Olive Parris was to give me the encouragement and support that enabled me to emerge from those troubled teen years and find my way at last.

For a start, I finally found a job that suited me. The employment office sent me to a man named Ignis Feig who ran an armature winding business called Carlin Feig, making and fixing electric motors and generators. Ignis was a former sergeant in the Polish army, and Jewish too, so he knew all about being an immigrant and a member of a minority group. He used to tell us stories about the war, and showed us the scars on his shins from injuries he received while blowing up a German tank.

Ignis employed four of us – three black guys and one Irishman – so we were all from minority groups. (I remembered those signs in lodging houses: "No Blacks, No Irish, No dogs." He never got the dog!) He had a good way of handling youngsters: he was generous, flexible and accommodating, and took time to explain the practical aspects of our work. There were no books – all the information came out of his head – so I was spared the classroom work I dreaded so much. In my previous jobs there had been no warmth and no encouragement, and also very little learning, because my employers didn't expect me to be able to manage much. Ignis's expectations were high. He believed in us and our potential, and we never abused the freedom and autonomy he gave us. That relaxed atmosphere enabled us to learn what was essentially a highly technical trade (we were learning electrical engineering, which should really have been a college course). His personal hands-on teaching style meant that all four of us blossomed. We discovered that we did have the ability to learn in an environment that valued us and built our self-esteem.

Outside working hours my life was better, too. Living with Olive Parris provided a calm and stable home life, and her infectious faith gave me a profound security, and a conviction that God had a plan for my life. I worked hard at my music, rehearsing, listening to Gospel records and learning to sing and play in that style, and I was rewarded by discovering that my practice enabled me to improvise and add to the worship experience for the people in church.

I travelled regularly with the church's team of evangelists, providing the music for services all over the country. Then one day Mum Parris told me that she was thinking of paying a visit to her childhood home in Jamaica – not as a tourist, but as an evangelist. She was planning to take me with her to provide the music for the revival meetings, and also a young lady called Sister Lyn, who had a wonderful testimony and a good singing voice. Jamaica is around a thousand miles west of Montserrat, so I wasn't exactly going home, but I hadn't been back to the West Indies since I came to England twelve years previously, so I was very excited. For weeks I dreamed of the sun and the sea, the simple outdoor life I'd lived as a child, and the taste of mangoes.

We arrived in Kingston late at night, and Mum Parris decided that we would stay with her brother in Browns Town rather than driving through the night to our destination. The house turned out to be in a slum area of the city, and I found myself sleeping on the floor in a shack with no running water and no hope of a shower in the morning. It was a rough area and I was kept awake by the heat, the unfamiliar noises and the discomfort of the concrete floor. I suppose I was very tired, but I worried all night. I had been so looking forward to this trip, and now I was hating it. Had I been fooling myself about my idyllic childhood? Had I forgotten what real life in the West Indies was like?

I was feeling very bleary-eyed the next morning when we set off, but with every mile my spirits rose. Once we were back in the rural areas I realized that life was very different there. As we drove through little villages with dirt roads and communal water tanks, looking so much more like the home I remembered, I felt a real connection.

We spent three weeks in Jamaica and I loved it. In the evenings Pastor Parris held revival meetings in tiny churches out in the countryside. Often the people would have walked a couple of miles in the dark to reach us, and they brought gifts with them – breadfruit and sugar apples. As they said, we had "come from foreign", so we wouldn't have had such treats for many years. In the daytime we did the sights, the Dunns River Falls and Montego Bay, which nowadays have become expensive tourist traps.

All the time I was reminded of home by the sounds and smells, and especially by the sight of the blue ocean, so different from the grey waters around England. We were in a hilly part of the country, and it was easy to climb to a vantage point from which we could look out and see the sea breaking on the rocks of Portland. My favourite drink was coconut water (made from a green coconut fresh from the tree), and I must have downed about five in a row on that first day. It was the taste of home, cold and refreshing, and every time someone asked if I'd like another I just kept saying yes! I couldn't wait to swim in the river and go fishing in the old way, catching lobsters with my hands. I took some back to the house where we were staying, and Mum Parris cooked curried lobster for our supper – nothing ever tasted so good as that homely meal.

When we got back to the UK I was cherishing a new dream: I wanted to go back to Montserrat for a holiday. I hadn't seen my dad since I was nine years old, and now I was doing well at work and was bringing home a regular wage, so I could afford to pay for my own tickets. Olive Parris encouraged me to make the journey: she knew it would prove my independence to myself. Before I went to live with her I had no hopes or dreams for my life, but with her support I had turned into a hard-working, capable young man.

I was twenty-one when I flew alone to Montserrat, and Dad was so pleased to see me. He had a new wife and two more children, so I couldn't stay in our old house, but my half-brother Joseph (nicknamed Fenton, he was another of Dad's sons by another wife) was living nearby, and I stayed with him. I hadn't seen much of Fenton when we were children – he lived with his mum and other siblings in Trants Village, close to Dad's cotton fields – but as we grew into young adults, we became much more aware of the importance of our various blood ties, and we made a point of getting in touch regularly. Fenton never moved away from Montserrat, but he went to work for an airline and got lots of free flights, so he was often able to come to the UK and visit me.

Once again, when I got home to Montserrat the first thing I wanted to do was to go swimming. Even when I was settled in the UK and thought of it as home, the river was the one thing I missed, and I used to think of it with a pang of homesickness. Its cool waters seemed to hold all my memories of childhood happiness, and the fun I'd had with Errol and the other boys as we splashed around, with water droplets sparkling in the sun and running off our dark skins.

So on the second day of my stay I said to Fenton, "I don't see anyone going to river."

"No one does it now," he said.

"I've not eaten river fish for so long," I said. "Can we go catch some?"

Fenton said it was a part of the village culture that was dying – nowadays people could get frozen food from the USA, and no one went swimming to catch their own fish any more – but he humoured me and fetched an old paint can. For me it was the moment when I finally reconnected with my youth. There was a winding path from home to the river, and I was conscious of wanting to set my feet in the exact places where I had walked before, and tread in my own childhood footsteps. I could see how over time the geography of the stream had changed slightly, the meanders cut deeper into the valley, and I realized how clear my memories were of this special place. I knew the water would be breathtakingly cold, because it came straight down from the mountain, but I couldn't wait to plunge in and swim, diving down through the clear water to the rocks, and feeling with my hands to catch the shrimp that darted out from underneath. As a boy I must have spent untold hours doing just this, and for a while I was back in my childhood again.

We spent two hours there, and in that time we filled the tin with lobsters and river shrimp. On the way back home we passed Dad's house, and he saw us through the open door.

"What yu got dere, Charlie?" he asked.

"Jacktumpy," I called back.

"Right! Well, call me when yu done cookin'," he said. He hadn't eaten river shrimp for a long while, either.

Fenton gathered together some breadfruit, green bananas and other vegetables, cooked up a stew – all the men in our family could cook – and went up the lane to call Dad. By then Dad's wife had cooked his dinner, but Dad left it on the table (I don't know how she felt about that!) and came to eat the fish stew with us. We had bowl after bowl, and at the end he sat back and belched – a compliment to the cook in West Indian culture.

"I tank God for dat," he said. "I haven' had a meal like dat in years."

It's a fond memory of my dad, and I'm so glad we shared that meal.

By this time I was twenty-one, settled in London with a skilled job, and musical director of Olive Parris's church. My friends, my work, my church and social life were all in the UK, but at heart I was still a proud Montserratian. The nine years of my early life in Montserrat laid the foundations on which my character was built, and formed my attitude to life's struggles. Nothing in Montserrat came easily, and you knew that whatever you got was achieved by hard work and determination.

I only ever had one experience of being on the dole, when I was unemployed at the age of sixteen. I found going to the benefits office was humiliating – I didn't like the way I was treated or the way I was spoken to, but most of all it felt like begging. I never went back, because I knew there was self-respect in making your own way in the world. My reaction, I'm sure, came from the attitudes instilled in me by my dad. He was proud that he relied on his own labour to provide a good standard of living for his family, and he wouldn't tolerate any kind of laziness, or asking for handouts or help. He believed that if you were healthy you could always get a roof over your head, water to drink and food to eat. Luxuries were unimportant, and you should put all your efforts into providing the necessities of life, and be content. He was known for his work ethic: if there was a strip of land around the house, it was never overgrown – he would clear it and plant food crops to feed his family. It was this emphasis on the importance of work that shaped my outlook, and Errol's too: neither of us can ever sit back and wait for handouts. We have to be proactive, working hard to achieve our aims.

The year I turned twenty-two I was happier than I had been for a long time. I had a good job, a good home, and a lively and fulfilling church life. At first we lived in Lower Clapton. The church had bought an old vicarage, and some of the skilled builders in our congregation had carefully dug out and repaired the cellar so that it was warm, dry and high enough for us to turn it into our church meeting room. We worshipped there for several years.

Sundays were great days: Mum Parris would be up at 6 a.m. to start preparing the Sunday lunch – a banquet of rice and peas (a favourite West Indian dish), stewed or roast chicken, oxtail, fried plantain, roast potatoes and salads. The scent of thyme and garlic would float up the stairs and make my mouth water. Sunday lunch for West Indians is the meal of the week, a family time that generally fills the gap between the morning service (from 10.30 a.m. till around 1.00 p.m.) and the evening service (which began at about 6.30). People would arrive early for Sunday School before church, and as we had plenty of space there would be classes for adults and children all over the house.

Pastor Parris was ambitious for her church and for the music we performed in it, and our favourite style was American Gospel. She knew that in the USA the recognized instrument for this style was the Hammond organ – an electronic organ invented by Laurens Hammond in the 1930s. It was originally designed as a cheaper alternative to the traditional mechanical pipe organ, but in the 1960s it had become a standard keyboard instrument for jazz, blues, rock and Gospel, as well as church music. I had never heard of any churches in England having one, but Mum Parris was in tune with the practice in the USA, and felt that this was what the church (and I, as the musical director) needed.

Even though we only had a cellar to meet in, she was determined to make it happen somehow, so she went to Boosey and Hawkes, the music shop in Regent Street, and explained where the organ had to go. She took with her all the measurements of the doors and the cellar steps, and the company agreed to take on the challenge. They cut the organ in half and rebuilt and rewired it, so that the top could be lifted off the base and carried down separately, rather like an Edwardian yacht piano.

I was ecstatic. The Hammond organ was completely different from a piano – as well as a keyboard it had "drawbars" which were like the stops on a pipe organ, giving dozens of different tone combinations, and also volume controls, vibrato and chorus effects and percussion settings. It also had pre-set combinations, so you could change from one to another rapidly. It was a serious piece of equipment, costing around £2,000 (a huge amount of money in the early 1970s). Even large churches were unlikely to invest that much money in their music ministry, but Olive Parris's vision was not to be denied. She was convinced that I had to develop my gifts and serve God through my music.

Over the next few years, although I was still working at the armature winding job, I spent all my spare time either rehearsing, practising, or performing in church. It was great to be part of a team working together for God's kingdom, bringing the good news to people and sharing in worship. Church had always been a part of my life – my mum always insisted that we went to church as a family, though when I was a child I didn't always pay much attention. But somehow I learned the basics of my faith through sheer repetition, and I found as I grew up that it was an important part of my existence.

It was also part of my West Indian culture: you work all week, you party on a Saturday, but on Sunday you go to church, and soak up the atmosphere of faith with all the others of your community, singing, praying, hearing testimonies, and just sitting and listening to the stories of Jesus. It was like resting in your faith. I never had any startling Damascus road conversion. For me it was like growing up in a family, and knowing that Jesus was my Saviour from my earliest days. On any Sunday you might hear from one or two people who had had a special experience of God, and those experiences taught and nurtured you. You might feel curious – maybe your turn would come when there would be some startling manifestation of the Spirit in your life – but meanwhile you were happy to be part of it. I knew that God was working in me, quietly, and I was doing my part by working as hard as I could to practise and develop the gift that Olive Parris had seen on that day when she laid hands on me and prayed for the anointing of the Holy Spirit.

By this time I was developing a reputation as a serious Gospel music artist in the UK, and was quite well known among the many churches we visited. Our church was still called by its original name, The Latter Rain Outpouring Revival, and our choir was known as the LROR Choir. Those twenty-five singers (sixteen women and nine men) were to become the core of the London Community Gospel Choir in the future. Mum Parris was always ahead of her time. While other Christian organizations tended to go around ministering to the churches, she had picked up ideas from the American evangelists she had met, and she took the message out onto the streets, to people who wouldn't usually go to church. She put advertisements for her events in newspapers and even on buses, and the result was that even when we were holding meetings in predominantly black churches, large numbers of outsiders, including a sprinkling of white people, would come along.

We also held revival meetings in London town halls, which were often rather grand places which could hold hundreds of people – in Hackney, Hornsey, Islington and Shoreditch. These were big occasions, and very exciting for the singers. We had a Junior Choir, whose enthusiastic mothers made their uniforms. These were simple but always colour coded: red tie, black shirt and black trousers for the boys, red blouse and black skirt for the girls. Sometimes they wore all white, or black trousers/skirts and white tops. At first the Senior Choir did the same, but then we decided to get robes made – copying the visiting American Gospel choirs we had seen. We liked their performances and the way they looked. One set of robes was maroon with gold trim on the sleeves, and a pleat at the front with gold fabric inside, so that when you moved there was a dramatic flash of gold. We didn't move around a lot in those days – our performances were quite restrained, and we hadn't yet begun to develop the complex choreography we now use.

At the core of all our success were the two elements of faith and hard work. We trusted that we were doing God's will, helping people to worship and bringing them closer to him. For me especially these were years of hard graft, leading the choir and accompanying them, but learning too. I never had a music teacher other than the Holy Spirit, and I had to trust in God's anointing on my life. I knew that music was a gift from God, but my background – and the voice of my hard-working Dad in my head – said, "And now it's your responsibility to develop it." My fingers wouldn't move by themselves: I had to train them. So I sat up late at night listening to Gospel albums, analysing how the harmonies were structured, then going down to the church and locking the door behind me and practising, practising, practising.

By this time our church had grown, and when there were over a hundred people in the cellar it could be sweaty and a bit claustrophobic, so it was time to relocate. We needed more space, more light and air, and so we sold the vicarage and we moved to a new building in Hoxton. I was still able to get to and from work easily, and I still had easy access to the church for my late-night practice sessions.

Those were good times. There was a Greek lady in our church named Marigula, and she loved the vibrancy and joy of our meetings. She was filled with enthusiasm, and wanted us to visit her home village and bring our music and teaching there. Pastor Parris agreed, and once again the team made a trip abroad. It was an amazing experience for me. I had travelled abroad before, but that was back home, to a culture I knew well. This was a different part of Europe and quite outside my experience. I tasted new foods and wines, saw people treading grapes in the traditional way, and then saw the unprocessed, cloudy grape juice brought to the table in a bottle. It was like a hard-working holiday, and I drank in the new experiences and opened my mind to a different language, food, lifestyle and culture.

Not long afterwards we made a similar trip to Bermuda, an island isolated in the middle of the North Atlantic. This was another culture shock: I had expected it to be something like home, but Bermuda is very much an ex-slave colony. The people have African origins but are much more American in culture than those in the West Indies. I made some good friends there, and later went back alone for a holiday. I was beginning to be a man of the world, with a broader experience and understanding than I had ever had before.

The one great lesson I learned was that whatever the culture, our message of hope and salvation travelled well. The words might have needed translation (as when Marigula translated the prayers and teaching into Greek) but the music did not. It seemed to me that the message in the music communicated directly with the spirit, and even when people couldn't understand the words we were singing, our passion and faith and trust in God came through to our hearers. I began to understand how powerful a tool I had been given for building faith.

I spent most of my time behind the organ, accompanying the singing, whether we were leading meetings in foreign countries, in London town halls or in our own growing church. During our outreach meetings, there was usually one person – called the song leader – responsible for the devotional part of the service, introducing the songs with a few words and leading the singing. One day our song leader didn't turn up, so Mum Parris suggested that I went forward and took over. Fortunately we had a second keyboard player with us, so he took my place at the organ and I went forward and led the congregation in singing the choruses, and did some singing myself. The song leader never came to that event, so I had to carry on all week. I was nervous at first about taking on the role – I was used to leading the choir, but they were people I knew, rehearsing in our home church. Standing up in public and speaking about the songs, and leading the singing, made me feel very exposed.

Our Pastor, however, was never one to allow you to slip back into the shadows when she had seen you achieve something. She followed up by asking me to start preaching, too. I found that really challenging. I had listened to a lot of Pentecostal preachers in my time, and I knew they generally had one shared characteristic: they spoke for a long time! Many of them prided themselves on never preaching for less than an hour, but they mostly achieved this by repeating themselves. They had generally covered everything there was to say in the first half-hour, but then they would go over the same ground again and again. Of course, there were always some brilliant speakers who could teach for an hour and leave you wanting more, but they were scarce, and mostly I found long sermons a bit boring. But congregations expected an hour-long sermon, and felt cheated if the preacher spoke for less time. If you were brief, they assumed you didn't have much to say.

I thought this was a form of pride – it made the speaker more important than the message, so I resolved that I would be different. When I stood up, I warned people that I wouldn't be there for an hour. I said that I would read some Scripture and say what I felt God wanted me to say, and then stop. They didn't seem to object. At first I sometimes found it hard to select a subject for my sermon, but as I did it regularly, it became easier.

I started preaching once a month at our home church, which meant making time for reading, prayer and preparation. This was as well as practising, arranging music, training the choir, accompanying the choir in church, and travelling with Olive Parris to revival meetings at home and abroad. And doing my day job at the engineering works at Carlin Feig. It seemed that I had very little time for myself, and less for socializing, but I was young and energetic, and somehow I managed everything. Life was good, and fuller and more exciting and satisfying than I had ever dreamed it could be.

It was at this time, in my early twenties, that I had my first serious relationship. Pauline was a member of our church, she was musical, she was beautiful, and I fell head over heels in love. There wasn't much leisure in my packed schedule of work and rehearsal and church, but I spent every spare moment with her. We were young and perhaps a little naïve, but we were old enough to understand the consequences of our actions. After a few months of whirlwind romance, I went to Olive Parris with a shamefaced confession: Pauline was pregnant.

I don't know what I expected Olive to say – I knew her well enough to know she wouldn't throw me out – but I had put us both in a difficult situation. I held a prominent position in the church, and I knew people would be disappointed in me. I was disappointed in myself.

I was immensely tempted to try to conceal the whole business, but I couldn't lie to Olive, and I was prepared to take her advice. Whatever I did would reflect on her: I was her protégé – she had given me a home for the last five years – and I preached under her. I professed the Christian faith, in a church which taught the value of chastity and expected its leaders to set an example, and I had failed, spectacularly and publicly. It was difficult to know how to deal with such a challenge to her leadership: some church members might support me, but it was entirely possible that I was bringing down a wave of disapproval on our heads.

Fortunately Pauline conducted herself with dignity, and I could never regret the birth of our beautiful son Marlon, but it was a difficult time. It was one of the first challenges to my faith: can belief in God really help us to overcome our failings? Mum Parris's advice was to admit everything – but would admitting it mean that I had to leave the church? Would I have to give up on my dream of being a musician? Were all my hopes and aspirations going to come to dust?

Mum Parris didn't think so. She thought that the less fuss we made, the better. She encouraged me to hold on to my faith and continue to trust in God, and not allow this failure to turn me aside from what God had set me to do. She reminded me that God's love is constant, and not dependent on us living perfect lives – everyone has some failures. She suggested that I stood down from preaching, but that I should continue playing my music. I think she knew that if everything was taken from me at this stage of my development, it would cause me to leave the church entirely, and find other things to do with my life. She was probably right: if the church had rejected me, I would certainly have given up on church, and possibly on my faith and my calling as well.

I believe that she showed great wisdom. She was a church leader, and she had to uphold the church's teaching – but she also wanted to keep my life going in the direction she believed God intended. In that, she has probably been the most important and influential person in my life. My blood mother had birthed me, but Mum Parris had parented me in so many ways, over and above what anyone might have expected in a church minister.

It all turned out well: Pauline and I are still on good terms, Marlon has grown up knowing me as his dad, and I've been able to share in his upbringing. This crisis could have thrown me off track, and I see it now as the challenge that comes with any gifting: do you have the determination to go on or will you be deflected? This kind of testing shows up our humanity – after all, God gives his gifts to humans, not super-humans. If we can hold on to our faith in God and remain steadfast, in spite of personal flaws and

My mother, Cyntilya Meade.

My father, Fenton Kirwan, in front of our house in Montserrat.

Me and my "mum", Dr Olive Parris.

Many people assume "Rev" is a nickname – I was actually ordained into the ministry!

At our debut concert I wore my "famous" sky blue Italian suit – it was the height of fashion and even years later I struggled to throw it out!

The London Community Gospel Choir's first concert at Ken... 1983.

This was the cover of our first single "Fill My Cup".

One of the many Hammond organs I have
played over the years.

Me and my eldest son, Marlon.

Marlon plays keyboards in church.

Our first Bass player, Dennis Barratt, who sadly passed away some years ago.

Vernetta, Leonn and Stephanie as children…

… and look at them now – all grown-up and all involved in music.

My youngest daughter, Ce'anna.

Our look has evolved since 1983!

This is what most people expect a gospel choir to look like!

LCGC has always had a very special relationship with Scotland and its residents – we even have our own tartan which I am modelling here outside Glasgow Concert Hall.

After nearly 30 years – singing still fills me with joy.

LCGC definitely keeps me young.

failures, we can achieve great things.

What it taught me, in the long nights of agonizing over my own frailty, was the nature of forgiveness and restitution. God doesn't say accusingly, "You've failed," but rather, "Are you willing to admit your fault, say sorry, pick yourself up and go forward with me?"

CHAPTER 5

Let my people go

When I began singing Gospel songs as a child, I knew very little about their origins: they were just the songs that my people sang in church. As my musicianship developed, I began to be able to differentiate between styles of music, and I recognized that there was a real difference between "our" songs in the black-led churches and those sung in the European churches around us. I started to wonder about the history and background of black music.

Gospel has its roots in Africa. From the seventeenth century until the nineteenth, the slave ships plied their trade on the triangular course from America and the West Indies, loaded with cotton, sugar, rum and other produce, to Europe where the goods were sold, then down to Africa where they picked up a cargo of men, women and children, and back across the Atlantic to America where the unfortunate Africans were sold as slaves.

Most of the Africans had never seen a white man before, and understood nothing that was said to them. They travelled in conditions of indescribable brutality and squalor, and up to half of them were expected to die on the journey. Only the strongest survived, which suited the slave-owners who bought them to work on their plantations. They had no interest in where their slaves had come from, so any plantation could include men, women and children from several different tribes. With no common language they were unable to communicate with each other any more than with the owners, until they learned to speak English. Once settled in their new homes and forced into obedience by whips and chains, the only expression they had in common was their native music. Contemporary descriptions by travellers in Africa reported that music played a vital role in communal life and especially in religion: public events would be celebrated by singing and dancing, accompanied by drums and stringed instruments made from gourds. The elements of early slave music seem to reflect this African background, with its drums and rhythmic dances, and the humming and high-pitched ululations that could be found all over the continent.

The simplest kind of music on the plantations was the "holler" – a kind of extemporized song where one worker would lift his voice in a long musical shout. The call would fall and rise, sometimes into a shriek, and consisted of strung-out words. Sometimes the song would include complaints about the work, the lack of food or other troubles, and sometimes it was used to let other slaves know where the singer was working. At intervals the singer would be urged on with cries and shouts from others working nearby, and this may have reflected a familiar song pattern of call and response.

Work songs were another identifiable format, used (like sea shanties and other songs in work environments) to synchronize physical movements when slaves were working together in a group or work gang. Slave owners liked their slaves to sing lively songs which set a fast tempo for the work. At harvest time, often several plantation owners would gather their slaves together to work to songs like "Shuck that corn": one would sing a line about the harvest feast, and others would join in with the repeated chorus:

All them pretty gals will be there
Shuck that corn before you eat
They will fix it for us rare
Shuck that corn before you eat
I know that supper will be big
Shuck that corn before you eat
I think I smell a fine roast pig
Shuck that corn before you eat.

The slaves made up their own songs for other reasons, too. They complained about their treatment:

We raise de wheat
Dey gib us de corn
We bake de bread
Dey gib us de crust…
We skim de pot
Dey gib us de liquor
And say dat's good enough for nigger.

Or they made fun of white people:

Poor massa, so dey say
Down in de heel so dey say
Got no money so dey say
Not one shillin' so dey say
God A'mighty bress you so dey say.

There is evidence that the call and response form, especially, is of distinctively African origin, and missionaries working in many different parts of the continent have reported hearing groups of singers engaged in this: the leader supplies the new lines, and the chorus responds each time with a repeated refrain.

When slaves were converted to Christianity, new concepts of God's love and mercy entered their songs. Some of these ideas spoke to their hearts especially. For instance, slaves dreaded being sold, wrenched away from their families and friends, and taken miles away by their new owners. As they watched their loved ones being led away, they would sing of the only hope of reunion they had:

When we all meet in heaven
There is no parting there.

Many slaves came to faith at the camp meetings which were a feature of two periods of revival, known as the Great Awakenings. The first of these swept through America in the 1750s, and the second in the 1820s and 1830s. These meetings were led by inspirational preachers, and the crowds attracted to hear them were so huge that no buildings could hold them. Instead, people would gather outdoors, sitting on planks for benches, facing a raised stage. Behind them would be hundreds of tents, pitched close together, because the meetings would go on for several days.

These meetings were popular with black slaves (not least, probably, because they offered some respite from work), and owners encouraged them to attend, doubtless in hopes of gaining a more willing and obedient workforce. The blacks were allowed to pitch their tents behind the preacher's stand, and join in with the singing.

There were no hymn books available for such large numbers of people, and in any case many of the labouring classes, white as well as black, were unable to read. So the preachers would revive the old practice of "lining out" – singing a line of a song and waiting while the congregation repeated it. Often they invented their own hymns, taking phrases from existing songs and simplifying them to provide an easily memorized refrain. They worked in texts from the Bible, and set them to popular tunes which they knew would be familiar to the congregation.

The slaves, segregated out of sight, joined in enthusiastically, sometimes spontaneously contributing their own songs, made in the same style. There was disapproval in some quarters when these songs began to be taken up by the whites and sung in their own churches. They became known as "spirituals", from the biblical command to use "psalms, hymns and spiritual songs" (Ephesians 5:19).

Churches were segregated, too, of course. Landowners considered it their duty to ensure that their workers received religious instruction, and everyone would attend church on Sunday, with the slaves sitting together at the back. There they learned some of the hymns sung by their white owners. Nevertheless, their instinct was to worship in a different, less inhibited manner. Their native African religions expressed themselves in singing, shouting and exuberant dancing – behaviour unacceptable in the sober Protestant tradition.

Because they wanted to worship in their own fashion, the black slaves were often allowed to hold their own services on Sunday evening, after they had finished their chores. There they would sing their own songs, listen to one of their own number preaching or reading (if anyone was literate), and praise God in their own ways. One of these practices was known as the "shout": the benches would be pushed back, and the congregation would gather in a circle. A spiritual was sung, sometimes by the dancers, sometimes by others standing by, and the slaves began to walk or shuffle round in a ring. The style of movement was a jerking, hitching motion, and could be very energetic and go on for a long while, with shouting, clapping and stamping. The shout was common in the Southern states, and though many slaves considered any form of dancing to be "sinful", the shout formed a sanctified form of dance when used in worship. If you watch it today, it's quite extraordinary to see the vigour of even the largest or most elderly people: you might see them hobbling into their place in church, and think that they can scarcely walk; then the shout begins and they are pounding the floor and moving as fast as the most agile of their companions.

However, meeting in the white man's church, or even in their own "praise cabins" on their home plantations, they still felt inhibited by their owners nearby (or sometimes sitting in state in the meeting). So occasionally they would hold prayer meetings late at night, out in the woods and hidden away from the main farm. A field hand singing as he worked, "Steal away to Jesus" or "When I went down in the valley to pray" was announcing a secret late-night gathering to his mates.

Black people were not allowed to form their own independent churches until the late eighteenth century. Their first hymn book was published in 1801 (*Collection of Spiritual Songs and Hymns Selected from Various Authors*) and included hymns by Isaac Watts and John and Charles Wesley, with the simple folk-tunes popular at the revival meetings, but the later editions also included spirituals.

Many spirituals retained the motif of the repeated refrain, and were often based on lines from more traditional hymns. An image from Isaac Watts' verse

When I can read my title clear
To mansions in the skies

emerges in a new form:

Good Lord, in the mansions above
Good Lord, in the mansions above
My Lord, I hope to meet my Jesus
In the mansions above.

The call-and-response format could be infinitely elaborated and used anywhere, in church or in the field. Other songs in this style included "There's a great camp meeting in the Promised Land" and "Sitting down by the side of the Lamb". Spirituals also used other styles: a slow, sustained melody (like "Deep River" and "Were you there when they crucified my Lord?") or a faster, syncopated rhythm ("Shout all over God's Heaven" and "Little David play on your harp").

Preaching and song were the media through which illiterate people had access to the stories of the Bible, and of course the stories which resonated most with the slaves were those of Israel's slavery and liberation. An obvious favourite was

Go down Moses
Way down in Egypt land
Tell ole Pharaoh
Let my people go.[6]

When the slaves sang "Didn't my Lord deliver Daniel – then why not every man?" or "Didn't it rain?" (in which God spares Noah, the righteous man), they were singing of their longing and hopes for freedom, as well as of salvation.

By the mid-nineteenth century a profound rift had grown up between the more liberal, better educated, industrial North of the USA, and the rural Southern states. The central issue was slavery, which the North believed should be abolished, and to which the Southerners still clung as central to their way of life. Long before the American Civil War of 1863, which finally decided the issue, slaves had been fleeing oppression in the South and making their way to the states of the Midwest which had been ordained free by 1787, or to the north-eastern and mid-Atlantic states where almost all slaves had been emancipated by 1800.

They were helped on their way by sympathizers who set

up a network of secret routes and safe houses, known as the Underground Railroad. Harriet Tubman, herself an escaped slave, worked on the Railroad, guiding first her relatives and then dozens of other slaves to freedom. She was also known by the codename "Moses", a fact which compels a different reading of spirituals such as "Go down Moses". Were those midnight praise meetings, held in secret, also used to plan escapes? Were the songs sung under the watchful eye of the overseer also used to pass on coded messages? "Sweet Canaan's happy land" may represent heaven, or it may mean the free states of the North, of which they sang, "I want to go home... Dere's no whips a crackin'... No more slavery in de kingdom... All is gladness in de kingdom." Songs like

Gospel train comin'...
Git on board, li'l children
Git on board
There's room for many a more

take on a different meaning in the light of the Underground Railroad. Even "Wade in the water" may be a reminder to the escapers that walking in the river shallows made it harder for the pursuing bloodhounds to follow their scent.

It was this background of oppression, despair and hope which gave the spirituals such depth of meaning when they were first introduced to the wider world.

By 1871 there were many freedmen even in the reluctant South (which, in the face of emancipation, established "Jim Crow" laws[7] which made the lot of the freed slave almost as hard as that of the unfree). The American Missionary Society had been busily setting up schools and churches for them, and in Nashville, Tennessee, it established the Fisk University. However, like many such educational establishments, it was desperately short of money. George White, the university's treasurer, was also its director of music, and he had the idea of starting a choir and taking it on a fund-raising tour. He selected twelve students for training, and put together a programme which included both spirituals and items from the standard classical repertoire.

Their first tour, in October 1871, was initially greeted with suspicion. America had seen black people on stage, but usually in "minstrel" bands, and the sight of smartly dressed young people singing mainstream music was a surprise. George White had arranged the spirituals into more formal harmonies, but nothing could disguise the singers' heartfelt enthusiasm for "their" songs – slavery was still a recent memory.

At first the group was advertised as "coloured students from Fisk University", but then White renamed them the Jubilee Singers (after the Jewish practice of celebrating a year of jubilee, cancelling debts and making a fresh start). The group was invited to sing in churches and at concerts, and money began to pour in for the university. By the following March it had paid off its debts and raised a further $20,000 for new buildings.

In 1873 the choir toured England, taking part in revival meetings and meeting their countrymen, Ira Sankey and Dwight Moody, whose slogan was "Mr Moody will *preach* the gospel and Mr Sankey will *sing* the gospel". Subsequent tours took in Europe, Australia and New Zealand and the Far East. The Jubilee Singers (and the many imitators who followed them) were presenting the world with songs from their own black culture. They were crossing the divide between black and white but also the line between sacred and secular, between singing the Gospel for its own sake in worship, and singing it in concert performances for money. It raised questions which are still debated today.

The development of Gospel was influenced over the next few decades by several strands of music. Throughout the nineteenth century white musicians had often "blacked up" to imitate the distinctive music heard on the plantations. The performances of these "nigger minstrels" caricatured the speech and manners of the slaves as well as their music. These groups in their turn were later imitated by black entertainers, and many of both kinds of groups began to include spirituals in their acts, in the wake of the fame of the Jubilee Singers. These groups helped to preserve spirituals at a time when the black churches were abandoning them, as they sought to integrate themselves into white society and adopt European culture. When the spiritual re-emerged as a popular form (sung by, for instance, Paul Robeson[8] in the 1920s), it was transformed by more sophisticated arrangements that were more acceptable to white sensibilities.

Another influence was barbershop quartets, started by the men and boys hanging around the all-male meeting place in African-American neighbourhoods, and singing informally together. Their spontaneous four-part harmonies became the source for the later Gospel quartets.

A third strand was Pentecostalism. After the Civil War the new black churches (mostly Baptist and Methodist) bore a strong resemblance to their white-led originals, but that was changed by the Holiness movement which sprang up. This emphasized not only salvation but "sanctification", the importance of living a holy life, achievable only with the leading of the Holy Spirit. The African-American culture was particularly open to this focus on the work of the Spirit and the gifts of speaking in tongues, prophecy and making a joyful noise, and the Pentecostal movement was born. New churches such as the Assemblies of God and the Church of God in Christ were also open to new ways of making music, and did not differentiate between instruments suitable for worship and those used in "sinful" secular performances, so they used pianos, guitars and percussion instruments which became such a feature of Gospel music.

This element was present in the West Indies, too. American preachers who had formerly been slaves were now free to travel, and many of them went to the West Indies with their message, holding camp meetings and teaching their brothers there. In this way the songs spread to all the islands, though sometimes with local variations of words and music.

The final influence was the birth of the blues, a form whose origin is hard to pin down. It may have grown out of the original field hollers, work songs and folk songs, but at a time when the black-led churches were most fiercely critical of anything outside the closed circles of religion, its subject matter was emphatically secular: love and loss, drinking, dancing, betrayal. The blues was moral in its way: it accepted that you reap what you sow, and that a life of debauchery would result in misery, but it had no place in the church. The blues was played in bars and taverns, and its mood was depressed rather than inspirational. Its subject matter may have caused it to gain a reputation as "the devil's music" – something which added to its attractiveness in some quarters – but inevitably there were some singers who attempted a fusion of the styles. The blind guitarist Willie Johnson (who was born in 1897) combined the blues style with the faith of the spirituals, and others who started out as blues singers came back to the church in later life. There was always exchange and interaction.

The term "Gospel music" was probably first used by Philip Bliss, who in 1874 published a collection called *Gospel Songs, a Choice Collection of Hymns and Tunes, New and Old, for Gospel Meetings, Sunday School*, and it soon became the term accepted and understood as a particular kind of song, easily learned and combining words and music with emotive effect. One of the most influential of the black Gospel singers was Thomas Dorsey, the son of a Baptist preacher and teacher, who first made his name as "Barrelhouse Tom", playing piano in dance halls. The invention of the phonograph and the various techniques of recording sound had opened up a wider market for all forms of music, and together with the singer Ma Rainey (known as the Mother of the Blues) and his own Wildcats Jazz Band, Dorsey began recording their blues performances.

In the early 1930s Dorsey returned to his religious roots and began writing and singing exclusively for the church. At the 1930 National Baptist Convention his song "If you see my saviour" was sung by Willie Mae Fisher, and Dorsey set up a stand and sold 4,000 copies of the sheet music. His dramatic song "Precious Lord, take my hand", written after the death of his wife and baby son, disturbed many churchgoers with its blues style. It was to become a Gospel classic, recorded by Gospel singers and secular artists alike, including Aretha Franklin and Elvis Presley. (On the day he was assassinated, Martin Luther King had asked for it to be sung at a meeting planned for that evening.) Dorsey was a prolific songwriter, producing around 800 songs, and many of them, such as "Peace in the valley", became famous. In 1932 he established not only the Dorsey House of Music (which published around 500 of his songs and was devoted entirely to the promotion of black Gospel) but also the National Convention of Gospel Choirs and Choruses. Dorsey lived until 1993, so he saw the results of his trailblazing: a new style of Gospel song, music publishing companies to market sheet music, recordings of famous singers, networks of churches willing to experiment with new forms of music, and the conventions which brought them together.

There followed many notable soloists: Sallie Martin and Theodore Frye toured with Dorsey, demonstrating his songs. Mahalia Jackson was a dignified Baptist contralto who signed with Decca Records in the late 1930s; although she mainly performed in concert halls, she saw singing Gospel as an act of worship. She was the singer asked to perform "Precious Lord, take my hand" for Martin Luther King, and she subsequently sang it at his funeral. Rosetta Tharp, on the other hand, was a Pentecostal who played an early form of rhythm and blues guitar and lived life in the fast lane. They represented the two directions of Gospel music:

Mahalia played the Newport Jazz festival on a Sunday, so it would be a church service rather than a performance; Rosetta was both a minister and an entertainer, gaining notoriety by performing in a New York nightclub and with a reputation for promiscuity. She was cited as a musical influence by Johnny Cash, Little Richard, Jerry Lee Lewis and Carl Perkins.

Rosetta's flexibility was followed later by Clara Ward and the Ward Singers, who sang anywhere they were asked. They reputedly had the first post-war Gospel record to sell over a million copies. Clara Ward was an influence on Marion Williams (who sang with her) and later on both Little Richard and Aretha Franklin. James Cleveland was also a major figure in the recording world, receiving four Grammys. In 1968 he set up the Gospel Music Workshop of America. Other legends of the 1950s and 1960s included Edna Galmon Cooke, Brother Joe May, Daryl Coley and Andrae Crouch.

From the 1920s onward Gospel quartets became popular (though the name can be misleading as it describes a style rather than the exact number of singers – quartets often grew to seven or eight performers). Groups had names like The Swan Silvertones, The Dixie Hummingbirds, and later The Mighty Clouds of Joy and The Fairfield Four. Most Gospel quartets were male, but female groups included The Davis Sisters, The Harmonettes and The Caravans.

Perhaps the most famous quartet was The Soul Stirrers, led by Rebert H. Harris and later featuring the legendary Sam Cooke. This was one quartet with five members, so the dynamic lead singer could be backed by full harmony. Many later rhythm and blues singers were inspired or coached by the Gospel quartets.

American Gospel of this period also featured choirs: the first professional black choir was the Wings Over Jordan Choir, founded in Ohio in 1935. Once they had gained a regular radio show they gathered a huge following, enabling them to tour the country and later the world. Early choirs had presented a restrained performance, emulating the classical choral singing of the European tradition, but James Earl Hines, directing the St Paul Baptist Church Choir of Los Angeles, introduced a different style. His emphasis on rhythm and hand-clapping drew in the audience, and his call-and-response extemporising recalled the enthusiasm and excitement of the old church meetings of the rural South. Suddenly choirs were lively again, picking up a wider repertoire from traditional hymns to contemporary Gospel, and their listeners would get out of their seats and join in. Their fame spread: the churches all had choirs who loved to sing Gospel, and the great church conventions offered opportunities for the best of them to become well known. James Cleveland, who was famous as a singer, songwriter and choir director, made his first choir recording in 1960. In 1968 he formed the Gospel Singers Workshop (now the Gospel Music Workshop of America).

By the end of the Second World War Gospel was big business; recordings and radio stations consolidated its popularity (in the 1950s the powerful commercial radio station WLAC in Nashville was said to be listened to by 65 per cent of America's black population). The post-war world was a different one in many respects. Black servicemen returned to the USA having seen the world, including places where segregation was not the norm. The black-led churches, which themselves were born out of the Civil War and the end of slavery, were well educated and well organized and able to lend their considerable weight to the burgeoning Civil Rights movement. Its most charismatic figurehead and martyr, Martin Luther King, was a powerful preacher and political leader, who quoted Gospel songs in his speeches. Many of the songs which had sustained the slaves in their quest for freedom were taken up and sung with fervour by black and white campaigners alike. Charles Tindley, writing in the first decades of the twentieth century, had published a hymn with the refrain, "I'll overcome some day". This was picked up and adapted (in the best traditions of Gospel) and re-emerged as "We will overcome", arguably the theme song of the Civil Rights movement. Other songs were used in the same way: "This little light of mine" and "We shall not be moved"[9] became popular, sung at meetings to inspire and motivate the protesters. The themes emphasized the theology shared by both black and white Christians: equality before God, the importance of steadfastness in the face of tremendous odds, and the assurance of God's help for the faithful. Even the sophisticated whites, who had largely discarded church teachings in favour of 1960s liberalism and free love, were inspired and moved by their fresh encounter with Gospel music.

It's around this point that British and American Gospel music could be said to diverge, though of course there was always interaction and exchange of influences and ideas.

American Gospel, as we have seen, was affected by American black culture – from Thomas Dorsey onwards, jazz and blues artists influenced and were influenced by Gospel musicians emerging in the churches. In 1967 the Edwin Hawkins Singers (originally the North Californian State Youth Choir of the Church of God in Christ) released an LP featuring a funk-style arrangement of "O Happy Day" which became a worldwide mainstream hit.

Meanwhile, a huge cultural change had been occurring in Britain, as the wave of immigrants from the West Indies reached its peak in the early 1960s. The revival meetings and vibrant youth work of the Latter Rain Outpouring Revival were mirrored in the black-led churches across the country – mainly in the cities which were the focus of immigration, but most of all in the capital.

However, "West Indians" were not a homogeneous group: all the islands had their own cultural identities, and brought their own variant musical influences to the mix – ska, bluebeat and reggae from Jamaica, soca and calypso from Trinidad and Tobago, and fusions and derivations from many other places. The black music developing in the UK absorbed all this as well as current pop (like the Beatles) and the jazz, blues and even country and western music crossing the Atlantic. A few West Indians made their way to the USA, of course, but on the whole American Gospel remained more inward-looking. The result was that Gospel in Britain developed and diversified to a greater extent than its US equivalent.

In the melting-pot of London, however much the churches deplored the culture of the secular entertainment industry, their music was affected by what their local musicians were listening to. Consequently, if you visited a church in Brixton where most of the members were Jamaican, you would find that the music had elements of reggae and ska; if you went to Dalston where more people came from Montserrat and Trinidad and Tobago, the music would have more of a calypso feel.

This was also true of the many groups that formed in the late 1960s and early 1970s. Pastor Anton LaTouche started a group called The Harmonisers which featured singers and (later) electric instruments; in 1979 they became one of the first black Gospel groups to play on the main stage at Greenbelt, the Christian music festival. Their style evolved over time from a Jim Reeves sound (mainly country and western) to a mix of rock, funk and reggae. Michael Martin, who managed The Harmonisers early in his career, went on to manage a contemporary funk Gospel band called Paradise, who sang with the US Gospel star Andrae Crouch in the early 1980s.

Other early groups who began to be accepted in the mainstream music scene included The Singing Stewarts (a Trinidadian family from a Seventh Day Adventist church in Birmingham who focused on Negro spirituals and traditional Gospel songs); The Soul Seekers from Calvary Apostolic Church in Camberwell, whose style was mainly country and western; The Heavenly Hopes (who came from various Pentecostal churches in South London); and the Persuaders, led by George Dyer from Montserrat, who mainly played reggae.

For all these, both church affiliation and country of origin were important influences: each group evolved its own style, emerging from its members' shared cultural and denominational backgrounds.

During the 1960s music had become an important evangelistic tool in the white churches as well as the black ones, and various organizations had sprung up to promote it. Musical Gospel Outreach, established in 1965, had its own label called Key Records – this eventually became Kingsway Music. Other Christian labels were Herald, Evangelical Recordings and ICC Studios (International Christian Communications). An industry infrastructure was developing.

The range of styles being exhibited in all these performances and recordings demonstrates the eclectic nature of British Gospel as opposed to the more immediately recognizable American Gospel sound. American Gospel achieved entry into mainstream entertainment much earlier than British Gospel. Although the USA is officially a secular nation with no "established" church, nevertheless Christianity seems to play a larger role in everyday life for ordinary people (churchgoing there is estimated to be twice the UK percentage). Perhaps there is less resistance in the USA to openly religious lyrics.

There may also be a difference in professionalism: many commentators mention slicker production values and more skilled performers: "In the States they've got far more quality singers. They have a vocal group tradition that stretches way back. In Britain we do not have that depth of singing ability, but we do have young people coming up in the churches who have been encouraged to play an instrument" (Michael Martin in an interview for *Buzz* magazine, 1982, quoted in Steve Smith's *Black British Gospel*, Monarch, 2009).

Again, this comes from fundamental differences. The USA has a far larger population from which to draw its singing talent.

Professionalism is a key issue, one which many of us were still struggling with in the 1980s. The American Gospel singers had been dealing with the sacred/secular divide from the 1920s onward, and the free movement between the churches and the entertainment industry was well established. In the UK it was still impossible to earn a living as a musician within the churches: your ability to play, sing or train a choir was seen as a ministry, not a professional skill from which you could make money.

It was easier for an African American church to decide that it wanted its choir to be trained by a professional musical director, and be prepared to pay for it. This is only now beginning to be an acceptable practice in the UK. Hence the American Gospel sound is richer, often demonstrating greater improvisation and vocal skills – the result of professional musicians devoting all their time to perfecting their Gospel music. Here in the UK many of us still have to divide our time between our Gospel music and secular bands and session work.

However, I believe that the most profound difference between British and American Gospel music lies in our different historical roots. Yes, the story of Gospel begins in slavery for all of us. But the ending of slavery was a long-drawn-out process: the Slave Trade Act of 1807 ended the slave trade (but not slavery) in the British Empire; slavery itself became illegal throughout the Empire in 1833; but it was not finally abolished in the USA until the end of the Civil War in 1865.

What happened after that is crucial: the scattered islands of the British West Indies remained under British governance. The few white plantation owners were paid compensation for the loss of their slaves; much of the land was divided into smallholdings and sold; and although the islands remained part of the British Empire until the twentieth century, many of them had considerable control over their own affairs, and the transitions seem to have been relatively painless.

The American experience was different. Even when slavery was abolished, stringent segregation laws relating to education and public places (including transport) were imposed in many states. There continued to be profound inequalities between black and white right up to the Civil Rights era of the 1960s and beyond. This resulted in continuing bitterness among African Americans who were still suffering oppression at the hands of white people.

I believe that this accounts for the distinguishing difference between American and British Gospel in performance. We know the history, we feel for all the generations of our brothers who suffered; many of us have had minor skirmishes with racist attitudes in England. But our parents and grandparents come from countries where their views were respected, where their vote counted, and where they knew themselves to be the equal of anyone.

Our African American brothers are still only one generation away from segregation, from having to take the back seat on the bus, from being excluded from white schools and universities. When a black American sings Gospel, he feels the pain with more immediate intensity and passion. It's the difference between singing from the heart and singing from the printed page.

CHAPTER 6

A change is gonna come

The late 1970s was a groundbreaking period for music in the black-led churches. A huge number of choirs and bands of all sizes sprang up, enjoying the new musical influences from our African American brothers across the Atlantic. The exciting new albums being imported were produced with American professionalism, and they stirred youngsters to want to create their own. Groups formed and reformed in new combinations – male and female, small and large, using different combinations of voices and instruments. It was a time of flux and energy in church music, and many of the groups were serving the big conventions organized by churches such as the New Testament Church of God, the Church of God in Christ, and the New Testament Assembly.

For a while I played bass guitar with The Persuaders (I was the only one who was not a member of the Dyer family), and later with The Overcomers, where Errol joined me, playing lead guitar. Victor Brown, the lead singer, was determined to make the group as professional as possible, and brought in George and John Dyer from The Persuaders to help coach the musicians. The Overcomers was one of the first groups to really break out of the church circuit and play other venues, like Ronnie Scott's, the All Nations Club and even American Air Force bases (through links with American Air Force personnel who were members of the Church of God in Christ). Their style was influenced by Sam Cooke (of the famous

Soul Stirrers), James Brown and Otis Redding – a fusion of soul, Gospel and funk.

There was always a lot of interaction between all the groups – all the musicians knew each other, filled in for one another at times, and generally moved around freely, sharing ideas. It was a very fluid, ever-changing scene. One of my friends at the time was Joe Pitt, the son of a bishop in a well-known apostolic church in South London. Joe was a keyboard player, and he had been invited to play with The Heavenly Hopes – he was the one who encouraged them to get national recognition by entering a TV talent show called *Opportunity Knocks*. They produced two albums before they disbanded in 1976.

After that, Joe wanted to form a group of his own, and began looking around for the key people on the Gospel circuit. Many bands at the time were just groups of friends who got together, with personal links more important than ability. But Joe wanted this to be a supergroup, made up of top-quality musicians. He wanted a dynamic front man, and singers, keyboard players and guitars, and he wanted the best. He knew that if he could assemble a team of musicians of this calibre they could make a real impact on the Gospel scene. The result was Kainos.

Our final line-up included my old friend Carl Boothe (who was now my brother-in-law, having married my sister Doreen) as lead vocalist, Joe Pitt on piano and vocals, my brother Errol on drums, Verl Beccan on guitar, Dereck McIntyre on bass, Keith Stewart on bongos and percussion, Joel Edwards on guitar, and myself on organ and vocals. (Not all our members went on to make a career in music: Joel Edwards was later to become Director General of the Evangelical Alliance, and subsequently International Director of Micah Challenge.) Like some of our heroes, we combined traditional Gospel with funk, a blend of soul music, soul jazz and rhythm and blues – the emphasis on rhythm from the drums and bass guitar makes it good to dance to. This was still somewhat controversial as far as the more conservative church members were concerned.

We thought hard before deciding on a name. Lots of other groups had church-friendly names with words like "soul", "heaven" or "joy" in them. Joel Edwards had played in a group called "Sounds of Zion". We wanted something more neutral. That was when Joel suggested "Kainos". No one knew what it meant, so he explained that he was studying New Testament Greek and that *kainos* meant "new" or "fresh" or "changed". We agreed that it felt right for us: we wanted a change in musical direction from the Caribbean and country and western styles that dominated music in our churches, and we wanted to develop our own style that would appeal to young people. As Christians, we all felt that our lives had been changed by our faith, so it worked on all levels.

We held our debut concert in the back hall of a New Testament church in Willesden High Street – and the young audience were beside themselves with excitement. Lots of them got up and started dancing in the aisles, in a manner that the church Elders had never seen before. (They were unlikely to see it again, either – it met with some disapproval and no such concert was allowed again for many years.) We had a rapturous reception from the youngsters, but the Elders were stunned. This music – a loud mix of Gospel and funk – wasn't their style, and they were shocked at the response it provoked. They were also confused by our image, because we didn't look like a staid church group: we modelled ourselves on the professional American music scene, so everything from our dress style (platform shoes, I'm afraid, but it was the late seventies) to our instruments (Hammond organ and Fender Rhodes keyboards) was associated with progressive secular music.

In 1978 Kainos even made an album – *Changing* was marketed on the reggae label Tempus – and in 1979 we played at Greenbelt, which was a prestigious venue, with its mix of religious and contemporary music. The festival was filmed and you can see a clip on YouTube. It was unusual for a UK band to be invited to play on the main stage, but that year both we and The Harmonisers were there, alongside big names like Larry Norman. We also played at the Dutch equivalent of Greenbelt, called Kaamperland.

Meanwhile, Olive Parris had started a Bible school at LROR. She had been the church's Pastor since its inception, and she knew that she needed to plan for the future. So she decided to train up some members for ordination – and that included me.

Ours was an active, growing church, in the centre of a wide-ranging ministry to the community, running meetings in town halls all over London. I was already responsible for preaching in church once a month, the same frequency as the Assistant Pastor, while Pastor Parris took the remaining services. I also preached at many of the out-of-church meetings as well as organizing and leading the music for the choir and the devotions. My confidence was growing, and gradually I came to share her vision for me as the next leader of the church, whenever she decided to step down from that role. Studying for the ordained ministry was the obvious next step.

The course lasted for two years, and there were about fifteen of us taking it. We studied the Bible in depth, and wrote essays – not an easy task for someone who hadn't enjoyed school very much! We would research different characters in the Bible, explore their relationship with God, and draw out the lessons we could learn from them. We were given topics to present to the rest of the class, and practice in preparing and delivering sermons. Most of all, Olive Parris taught the importance of our own personal relationship with God.

At the end of the two years several of my fellow candidates had dropped out, and others had decided that they were not yet ready to take the final step, so only three of us came forward to be ordained. It was a very moving ceremony, and care had been taken to make it more ceremonial than our usual informal services: everyone was aware of the need for dignity and solemnity. The church was packed with our own congregation and our many friends from other churches: I was well known in church circles because as well as leading the LROR choir, I often played at events held in other churches, so I had friends all over London. The ordinands all wore white robes and stood at the front of the church while members of our own congregation read passages from Scripture, culminating in the Great Commission of Jesus: "Go and make disciples."

Our church had connections with many other local churches, including the Baptists, Methodists and Pentecostals, so Pastor Parris was able to bring six other ministers together to endorse our ordination. They laid hands on us and prayed for our future ministry, and then we turned to face the congregation. It was particularly great for me, because as I looked out at all those friendly faces, there was one special to me: my new wife.

During this time I was still musical director of the LROR choir, so although I was committed to working with Kainos (we rehearsed every Saturday afternoon and performed at weekends), sometimes the band had to perform without me because I had choir duties to attend to. And of course there was still the day job, and I needed to have a personal life, too. It just had to fit around everything else. So I suppose it was obvious that when I met a girl, she would be involved with music and the church. Andrea had come along to a service in the basement church in Evering Road. Mum Parris was leading the service, and she spotted this beautiful girl enthusiastically singing along to one of her special songs, so she invited her up to sing with her. Mum's instinct was right – Andrea had a lovely voice – and after the service we introduced ourselves. We talked about songs, and I played the organ and we sang along together, and our shared interest in music sparked a deep friendship.

Andrea had come to England from Trinidad and Tobago to study nursing, and she was now working in the Whittington Hospital in

Highgate Hill. She became a member of LROR, and in our free time we went out together. We soon knew we were serious about each other, and in 1980 we married in Trinidad, surrounded by Andrea's family and friends. Sadly, none of my family was able to make the journey.

I had managed to save a fair amount from my wages over the years, so I could afford to put a deposit on a little house in Leyton: 298 Capworth Street. It wasn't in good repair, but we fixed up one room to live in to start with. I didn't know anything about building or plumbing, but we had the help of the skilled brothers in the church, and we quickly had the house put to rights. That was a good thing, because soon the children began to come along: Vernetta (named for Olive Vernetta Parris) was born in 1981, our son Leonn in 1983, and our youngest, Stephanie, in 1984.

The children were a great joy, and still are. Like any young couple, we struggled to manage financially, and to fit everything into our lives – work, childcare, and of course our music. For a while, Andrea went back to doing night duty as a nurse to help us make ends meet; I went over to piece work at the armature winding works, so I was paid by the job instead of by the week. It meant that I could arrange my own hours to a certain extent. Some days I would work from nine to five, go home to eat, and go back to put in extra hours in the evening. I was a fast, efficient worker, so I could get a lot done. Then I could choose to have other evenings, or even a couple of hours in the late afternoon, free for rehearsals or travelling to a concert.

The children were all musical. Vernetta was the first to develop a great singing voice, and she was often my guinea pig when I was writing and arranging music. We'd go down to the garage where I had my keyboard, and I'd have her singing the second harmony line as I worked out a new song. Sometimes Andrea would be calling her in for bed, and I'd be saying, "Just let me do this with her one more time!"

Leonn made a big impact as soon as he arrived. He was a hyperactive little boy – you needed eyes in the back of your head when Leonn was around – and he quickly became the choir mascot. At the age of eighteen months he appeared on stage at the Royal Opera House, at a concert for the Queen's birthday, dressed in a miniature copy of the choir costume, and shadowing the choir conductor's every move. Later on he decided he preferred drumming, and he would sit on the drummer's lap at rehearsals, holding his own little sticks. Andrea and I questioned our own sanity when we bought him his own drum kit. So did the neighbours: he had a ground-floor bedroom at the other end of the house, and he knew he wasn't supposed to play his drums in the early morning or late at night, but I was often woken at 7.00 a.m. by neighbours ringing the doorbell to say that Leonn was drumming again.

Stephanie looked the most like her mother, and like her she developed a wonderful singing voice. She looked like a little bird when she was born, and we called her "Tweetie Pie", after the cartoon, and she still uses "T'pie" as a nickname. She was always making up her own tunes from a very young age; when she was about four a friend (who was a professional in musical theatre) asked if she could test her: she found that she had perfect pitch. It's not surprising that Stephanie is a singer/songwriter now.

With all those singers and musicians in the house, life wasn't ever quiet, but it was wonderful. Because our lives were so bound up with the church and the choirs, the kids became very sociable and confident, knowing they were part of a huge extended family. The choir members were in and out of the house, and we always had people willing to babysit for us.

Several of our church members became almost members of our family. Our first lodger was Pauline Cummings. She was about eighteen, and she was going through the usual teenage thing of not getting on with her parents. She asked me (as youth director) if she could come and stay with us, and I agreed. Perhaps I should have consulted my wife first – but as it happened, everything worked out OK, as Andrea was pregnant with Vernetta at the time, and Pauline was able to help with the new baby: we used to call her Vernetta's spare mother. When Pauline married, a couple of years later, I was the minister who conducted the service, and Andrea decorated the hall for the reception.

No sooner had Pauline moved out than another lodger moved in. We first met Tony McKenzie when he was about fourteen: he, too, didn't get on with his mother, so he came to stay with us like a foster child (rather in the way I had lived with Olive Parris). He became an uncle – or nanny – to our kids. When he was an older teenager he would take the babies out for the day in a sling, complete with nappies and bottles and all the baby stuff he needed. Nowadays he is married with two grown-up children himself, and works professionally in child care, leading parenting courses, but he still finds time to help with the grandchildren. Tony is Stephanie's godfather, and when her own baby Asa was born seven weeks early, Tony took time off work to cook, clean, babysit and help her recuperate. I was away touring at the time and so was her husband Ayo, so it was wonderful to know that Tony was there to help Andrea look after her. Even now, if any of them calls (including Leonn), Tony drops everything to be there for them. He's been a wonderful addition to the family, and a fantastic example of caring, consistent, fatherly love.

While the children were still babies, we were pretty busy with Kainos and LROR, but a new idea was being hatched. Music had always been important in the black-led churches, and many of us as leaders emphasized the importance of musical training, and giving young people the opportunity to sing and play with other good musicians. I had several conversations along these lines with two friends: Delroy Powell (the son of the Bishop of the New Testament Assembly in Tooting, and founder of The

New Testament Assembly Choir), and John Francis[10] (from the Pentecostal First-Born Church of the Living God, leader of The Inspirational Choir). We were all passionate about music and involved in playing, singing, leading and organizing choirs in our own churches. My own assistant at LROR was Lawrence Johnson, and he and I worked closely together. The idea was born that we should arrange a concert for our united choirs, getting the maximum number of voices together. We thought it would be a celebration of singing, and a training opportunity for the singers – if it went well, we thought, maybe we could repeat it the following year. It was a fairly simple concept.

Unfortunately, we ran into problems almost immediately. As soon as we started rehearsing, some of the singers reported that the leaders of their "home" churches were unhappy with the idea of them singing elsewhere. Some had even threatened to "de-fellowship" them – exclude them from the church – if they continued. Others were just made to feel uncomfortable that they were being disloyal.

I was bewildered by this attitude, and I took responsibility for visiting the Pastors of the churches, to inquire courteously what the problem was. Some were evasive, saying that they didn't think the venture was "of God"; others said that they were concerned because we were all so young, and that there was no older person in overall charge. I suspected that part of it was insecurity: they had heard how popular our new music was, and how different it was from the traditional Gospel being sung in their churches, and they were worried that we were trying to lure their young people away. I tried to allay their fears, explaining that I thought it would raise the standard of music in all the churches if we got the best musicians and singers to share their expertise. I assured them that I had no intention of starting my own church – I was only trying to organize a concert – but I didn't succeed. Their minds were made up, and they issued an ultimatum to their young people: if they continued to sing in our united choir, they could no longer sing in the choir in their home churches. Many of our young singers succumbed to this pressure and regretfully left us. John Francis was one of these, and he and many of his choir members abandoned the idea of the joint concert.

I had already had some experience of the power of television: I'd seen what a difference it made to Joe Pitt and The Heavenly Hopes when they featured on *Opportunity Knocks*.[11] So when I was approached by a film-maker called Simon Heaven,[12] who wanted to film LROR for a documentary, I was happy to agree. His programme was called *We're Gonna Sing*, and it brought British Gospel onto the television screens of people who had never heard of it before. I knew it could only be a good thing for us to get more exposure.

It was at this point that I was contacted by Channel 4, who ran a ground-breaking magazine programme called *Black on Black*, presented by Trevor Phillips.[13] The programme included live music and they wanted some religious content for the Christmas show in December 1982. The LROR choir was already well known in the black community, due to Olive Parris's policy of running events outside the churches, I had a considerable reputation as its musical director and as a maestro on the Hammond organ, and of course we had already been seen on TV. Since so many of the LROR members were also singing in the united choir (which had been depleted by the loss of John Francis and others), I decided to use the new choir for the TV performance. At that stage the new choir had no name, and we appeared as the LROR Choir.

It was hugely exciting to appear on a live television show, and it gave our rehearsals added impetus. After the broadcast, too, we had many more people willing to join with us – they had seen what kind of music we were performing, and how enthusiastically we were received. Our debut concert was planned for May 1983, at Kensington Temple, Notting Hill Gate. We rehearsed hard, at first in the LROR in Hoxton, and later on in Caribbean House, a cultural centre about five minutes away. Soon our rehearsals became like mini-concerts themselves. Caribbean House was a busy place where people came to socialize with their friends. When they heard us rehearsing they would wander into the hall to listen, and before long the hall was full and people were spilling out of the doors, clapping and singing along. We might have been essentially a church choir, but we were singing in a style that was different from anything people had heard before from their local Gospel choirs.

By then we had decided on a new name for our united choir: The London Community Gospel Choir (LCGC).

Typical of the vibrant music scene in the early 1980s was the concept of a Gospel cruise. Ralph Weekes was a successful businessman who had come to England from Barbados when he was nine. He ran a cargo shipping company alongside a record label and a mission and outreach organization, as well as a Gospel group called Children of the Kingdom and a management, publishing and promotion company called Pure Gospel. In January 1983 Ralph laid on the first ever Gospel cruise, from Dover to Gothenburg, with live music on board. The churches supported it because they loved anything that would enthuse their young people, and Andrea and I were asked to lead the entertainment. The only problem was that Andrea was nine months pregnant with Leonn – but it was her first invitation to travel and perform as a guest artist, and she said, "I don't care, I'm going!" So we left Vernetta with Pauline and set off.

I had a great time on the boat, meeting people and talking music all day. Andrea gave a fantastic performance and sang in the morning service on the first day, and spent the rest of the trip in her bunk, struck down by seasickness! We thought she would be better when we got on shore, so we went sightseeing in Gothenburg, but she collapsed in the town and we had to get a taxi back to the boat. Still, our performance had been good enough to make several members of the tour – including Yvonne White, who had sung with the Gospel, funk and reggae band Echoes of Joy – ask if they could join LCGC. It seemed that everyone wanted to be part of the new choir.

Fortunately Andrea recovered quickly, and Leonn was born in February. Andrea, typically, supported what I was doing with the choir not only by running the home and caring for two babies, but by doing masses of organization and performing in the debut concert, too.

The birth of LCGC overlapped briefly with the life of Kainos, but I soon realized that I couldn't do justice to the band as well as running two choirs (Lawrence Johnson, my deputy at LROR, and I had together become the driving force behind LCGC). I gradually withdrew from Kainos, and the band itself disbanded amicably not long afterwards. There was one rehearsal when everyone was chatting, and Errol asked the crucial question, "Do we want to carry on?" He had realized that for him, rehearsing had become a chore, and he felt he had lost his initial drive and enthusiasm. His honesty enabled the others to relax and admit that they felt the same – they all had busy lives, with lots of other things going on. They were ready to move on; the band had done its job, playing an important role in introducing the fusion of funk and Gospel. It is still occasionally cited as having influenced subsequent Gospel bands, including the well-known Paradise.

I had always assumed that I could run the LROR Choir and LCGC in parallel (especially since LCGC was intended to perform a single concert!), but things didn't work out like that. The problems that John Francis and others had experienced in their churches began to be repeated in ours. It was a shock for Lawrence and me to realize that our own church wouldn't support our work with LCGC.

LCGC usually rehearsed on Wednesday evenings, and we

found that by Sunday, church members would be complaining to us about petty things – that the chairs hadn't been put back properly, or that there were scuff-marks on the paintwork. I had held a leadership position in the church for a long time, and I found it hard to believe that people who had joined the church long after me were so ready to criticize and find fault. It made me feel unsettled and unhappy, and I began to dread going to church on a Sunday to face the latest barrage of criticism. This was unheard of: I usually went to bed on a Saturday night looking forward to worshipping, to playing the organ as my way of serving God and my church. Now my heart was increasingly dejected: I found I just didn't want to be there.

Eventually matters came to a head. A lady who had recently joined the church had been appointed as caretaker, so she had the keys to lock up the building. One evening she was trying to hurry the choir members out, and was being quite rude to them. I confronted her about this, and asked her to be more polite, especially as many of the LCGC choir members were in effect visitors from other churches. In response she jangled the keys in front of my face tauntingly, saying, "I'm the one who has the keys, an' I can lock you out. You get out when I say!"

It was the last straw, and I decided that I would have to leave. I had served the church faithfully for so many years as an elder, a youth leader, a minister of music, choir director and worship leader. I couldn't cope with a relative newcomer pulling rank on me and being given the authority to harass me.

As I had always done with any church problem, I took my worries to Mum Parris, confident that she would give me wise counsel. My relationship with Olive Parris had been one of the most important in my young life. She had been not only an inspirational spiritual example, but also a mother-figure, giving me love and care and building my self-esteem so that I grew up to live and work as a husband, father and leader, and teaching me how to nurture other young people in my turn.

Perhaps the only area in which her selfless love had been lacking was in her ability to let go. Although she rejoiced with me when I married, she wasn't able to come to our wedding, and she found the separation hard when I moved out to live with Andrea and we started a family of our own. I think she had hoped I would go on being her "son" for a very long while, and perhaps she feared loneliness. In fact, after I left home, she unexpectedly announced that she was getting married too, so it wasn't as if she was entirely alone. I think that she needed someone to take care of, and my leaving home had left a vacuum which she tried to fill. Sadly, that marriage didn't last long, and I felt sad and slightly guilty that she was obviously so distressed by my leaving. I valued the love and security she had given me, and I knew I owed her so much, but I told myself that I had my own life to live. It's in the nature of life that the young move on to start their own lives, and I couldn't give up my new family to accommodate her. So there was already a little distance developing in our old, close relationship.

When I started rehearsing LCGC in my home church, it had never occurred to me that there would be any issues about it. I had thought that initiating the new choir would put LROR on the map as a progressive church that had nurtured the new music. I explained the recent events, and told Mum Parris how distressed I was. I was shaken when I realized that she had no intention of supporting me, and that she showed no regret at what was happening. She said she was concerned that LCGC was going to take Lawrence and me away from our duties with LROR – Lawrence ran the Junior Choir and I ran the Senior Choir. I agreed that I would be away occasionally, but pointed out that there were other young musicians coming along within the church, who were fully able to deputize for me.

Olive Parris had always been good at encouraging the youngsters in the church, providing us with good-quality instruments and opportunities to rehearse and perform and flourish. In particular, she had always encouraged me to improve my skills and to work hard, and to be ready to take the next step as God prepared the way for me. I was so sad that she couldn't see that LROR would be OK, and that LCGC was good for both of us. Her approval was important to me, and I would so much have liked her to endorse the work I was doing. But the sturdy independence and sense of responsibility she had developed in me meant that I wasn't able to give up on the project I had started. I had to carry on.

When I made the formal announcement that I would be leaving the church to pursue my work with LCGC, the congregation were shocked. Many of them pleaded with me not to leave, reminding me of all I had done, and saying that they already saw me as the next leader of the church. I pointed out that these protestations were all well and good, but that no one had supported me while I was being harassed because of the new choir. I wasn't prepared to have to fight to exert my authority in the church, and I would rather leave than cause bad feeling. I knew that God had anointed me and given me my musical talent, and I trusted that he would make it possible for me to use it. It seemed ironic that it was the conviction which Mum Parris had planted in me that was now taking me away.

Even when I was first playing in Kainos, I had faced some criticism and opposition because of the mix of traditional Gospel with other musical styles which seemed too secular and popular to be included in church music. To a certain extent it goes with the territory, and in some ways it's a good sign. People put up boundaries and feel secure inside them: "This style is religious music, but that style isn't." It's good to break them down and bring in a breath of fresh air. That's certainly what we found ourselves doing in LCGC.

It was sad that this departure soured the beginnings of LCGC, but in many ways it was part of the whole vision for change and renewal that affected our music. We needed to break away from the old denominational divisions and restrictions that bound us. We had never intended to start a new church of our own; our first two children, Vernetta and Leonn, were baptized at LROR, and Stephanie was baptized at the Elim church in Lewisham which we attended for a while. Eventually, however, Andrea and I started a small prayer group at home, which grew rapidly. We soon realized that this prayer group, together with the fellowship of musicians we worked with, was in effect a little church of its own, which we called The Agape Fellowship. As the ordained minister, my nickname, inevitably, became "Rev".

CHAPTER 7

Out of many, one voice

We had no idea, back in 1983, how big LCGC was to become. Many of us had been part of bands that came and went, bursting onto the music scene with enthusiasm and fading away as fast, as people moved on. If anyone had asked me, I would have said that LCGC probably had a life of around two or three years. After all, we founded it initially to get some choirs together for just one concert – and maybe another one, the following year. The real aim was to nurture singers and musicians and train them so they could take new skills and enthusiasm back to their home churches.

That first concert was an amazing experience. We had done hardly any advertising, other than printing a few flyers, but it wasn't needed: word of mouth had done our promotion for us, and the church was packed. For the first time we began to realize that we really were doing something new – and that LCGC had huge potential. Throughout the show people were on their feet clapping and dancing, only stopping for the more meditative and serious numbers. One of our unique qualities was the range of music we performed. We had already developed our funky, beat-heavy style from our experience in Kainos, but now we added more.

Andrea had been educated in a convent school in Trinidad and Tobago, which had always been the top performer in the local music festivals, so she had grown up with European classical music. She believed that our repertoire should be more eclectic, and she knew just the person to help us widen our range. Through a series of connections she was in touch with Wayne Marshall, a classically trained organist, conductor and pianist, and he agreed to come and help train the choir. So that first concert included not only spirituals and Gospel songs in our own style, but also music by Handel! Most of the choir couldn't read music, so Wayne was able to train them and provide the link between the singers and the unfamiliar style. Those numbers certainly added impact to our performance, and demonstrated the choir's ability to produce a truly diverse repertoire. We sang the Hallelujah Chorus, Negro spirituals, traditional Gospel songs and contemporary Gospel too. Most unusually, we also wrote and performed our own songs – few choirs included musicians who were proficient enough to compose. When we performed well-known songs, we also made our own arrangements, stamping them with our own style. It made an exciting programme.

The success of that first concert in May 1983 built on the exposure we had had in the Channel 4 programme the previous Christmas. Until then, church choirs had seldom performed outside their churches, but the response to the television show was amazing. Trevor Phillips was inundated with phone calls and letters from viewers asking for more of our type of music. For Easter 1983 he ran a competition: Gospel groups all over the country sent in sample tapes, and a panel of judges selected who would perform in an Easter special. The Church of God in Christ (COGIC) choir were successful, and also The Inspirational Choir, led by John Francis, who were spotted by the band Madness, and subsequently invited to sing on their "Wings of a Dove"[14] single. Suddenly Gospel was making the headlines. The moment was right.

The result was that instead of disbanding LCGC after one concert, or planning a second concert at our leisure, we immediately found ourselves deluged with requests for performances. My home address was the point of contact, and within weeks we had so much correspondence that we had to put a filing cabinet in the bedroom. It wasn't just local churches asking for us, either: we were playing at large London theatres, in concerts headlined by big names. In 1983, our first year, we supported The Mighty Clouds of Joy at the Dominion Theatre, London, and featured in the International Rock Gospel Concert at Wembley Conference Centre and in a concert called A Time For All (which was broadcast by Radio London) at the Queen Elizabeth Hall on the South Bank. Channel 4 filmed our Christmas concert at Kensington Temple for another edition of *Black on Black*.

One reason why we became established so quickly was the amount of time and effort Andrea put in. As a nurse she was used to being highly organized, and she brought all her planning skills and her energy to running the choir. She took a course on writing press releases so she could get items about our concerts into local papers; she went to the library and studied how music companies were set up; she rang up producers and got bookings for the choir to appear on TV and radio. Every appearance boosted our profile and made the next contact easier to reach, and before long our reputation spread simply by word of mouth.

I was still working at Carlin Feig, and Andrea was at home with the children, but increasingly we felt the pressure to be as professional as possible. We were being paid for performances outside church, and once money is involved it's vital that everything is recorded properly and that all the business dealings are transparent. Andrea got in touch with the Musicians' Union and learned all she could about establishing a company, how to draw up a contract, and how to set up good administrative systems (the ones she set up are still in place, adapted for use with computers).

The first time we entered a proper recording studio was to record "The Long and Winding Road"[15] with Paul McCartney at Air Studios in Oxford Street. Everyone was a bit overawed. How had we got here so fast? When we played the Royal Albert Hall with the legendary Al Green the following year, we were even more stunned. Al Green was named by *Rolling Stone* magazine as one of the "100 greatest artists of all time", and sold more than 20 million records. And we were an amateur church choir. It was crazy!

The only explanation was that our kind of music was something that the white community hadn't heard before, and they couldn't get enough of it. Until then, the only British Gospel singers who had mainstream success in the UK were a small group called Paradise who got a record into the Top 40. We were the first choir to get our name known.

In the early 1980s, in spite of years of immigration, most of "Middle England" outside the inner cities seldom saw a black face, and the media scarcely acknowledged the presence of the black community. There were harldy any black newsreaders or television personalities, few black sportsmen, and almost no dramas with black actors. That was why Channel 4's minority programming was groundbreaking. It was, however, not long after the race riots in Brixton and Toxteth, and what people *had* seen was extensive media coverage of black youths fighting with police. We showed a different face of black England: young Christians singing about our faith, talented, disciplined, working together and producing an amazing sound to praise and celebrate God. We began by unifying the black community, uniting so many doctrines from different churches, and focusing on what we had in common, our love of our Lord. Then we began getting these invitations to non-church events and festivals where the majority of the audience was white. Now we were opening doors and building bridges between black and white, too. Our motto was "Out of many, one voice".

For the young members of our choir, it was daunting. Almost all of them were from Pentecostal churches which in those days were known for their strict guardianship of their young people. Young Pentecostals did not go to pubs or clubs, they did not dance, and the girls never wore trousers, only skirts of a demure length. They wore no make-up, and any kind of hair processing (like having their tight curls relaxed into glossy ringlets) was frowned upon, and likely to be singled out for censure in the Members'

Meeting. Attitudes have changed in most churches since those days, but back then you didn't even visit another church unless the meeting had been arranged with the blessing and supervision of your Pastor. Now I had collected a group of youngsters from a lot of different churches, and every weekend I was traipsing up and down the country with them in a coach, taking them who knew where. No wonder the Elders disapproved. A couple of our members found their leadership roles in their churches being removed from them: Jenny LaTouche was told that she could no longer be the Sunday School Superintendent, because of her "disloyalty" to her church.

Nevertheless, very few people resigned from the choir. Our members believed that they were doing God's will and taking his name out into the world, and they were willing to work hard for the privilege. Most of them were single (for a long while I was the only married member) and young – the oldest were only twenty-three or twenty-four. Most of them had jobs and the rest were students. Yet they came faithfully to the Wednesday rehearsal every week, and performed almost every weekend, covering hundreds of miles in our two coaches. Often we would drive back late at night after a Sunday evening show, arriving in London at 4 or 5 a.m. on Monday morning, with just time for a shower and breakfast before setting off for work.

In 1984 we appeared on TV-am.[16] If you look at a video of that show, you can see how inexperienced the choir was. Everyone had firmly refused the offer of make-up for the cameras (the girls were almost as scandalized as the boys by the suggestion), so their faces look blank and washed out by the lights. Even worse, they all look terrified! Lawrence Johnson, the choir director, is waving his arms and trying to get them to move around and look as though they're enjoying themselves, but they're all standing rigidly to attention. The sound, however, is magnificent. Their voices blend beautifully, and there's no doubting their sincerity.

The other type of request we started receiving was to sing at weddings. Our first was for Dawn French and Lenny Henry in 1985; since then we have sung at dozens of celebrity weddings, from David Yates' (best known for his work on the Harry Potter films) to Wayne Rooney's. Nowadays we offer a wedding service – with a wide choice of songs, size of group, and costumes (formal, informal, or choir robes). It's very popular.

In those early days, conscious that we were missing out on services at our home churches, we decided that we needed a chaplain, so we appointed Reverend Dennis Scotland to travel with us. One year he was asked to speak at Greenbelt, the great Christian rock festival, and he wanted us to lead the singing. So a small group of us went up the night before and slept on the floor of the marquee where he was going to speak. The next day we looked out at the huge audience in amazement; we never dreamed that one day we would be playing on the main stage. Soon we were playing at Glastonbury, too – something we now do every year. One summer it rained so heavily that our bus got stuck in the famous Glastonbury mud. A tractor came to tow us out, but unfortunately the driver fastened its tow-line to the fuel pipe, which tore off and spread diesel everywhere. It's not exactly a glamorous lifestyle, coming off stage and wading around in a mix of mud and diesel!

We still have a chaplain (at the time of writing it's Sue Viner, who sings with us, too). We like to have someone whose main job is to keep an eye on the choir's spiritual welfare, who can lead our times of devotion and be responsible for pastoral care. I would like to do it, but I have so many things to do, especially when we're travelling, that I know it would get crowded out of my schedule, and I believe it's too important for that.

It's a fantastic experience to play at rock festivals with mainstream artists. Most of them have never come across a Christian backstage, so they're a bit confused when they pitch up and find about forty young people having a prayer meeting before they go on. They get used to us, and we have noticed how often some of them arrive early and hang around in the area we've been given, just soaking up the atmosphere of prayer. They might never have set foot in a church, but they obviously find it strangely attractive, and they want some of the mixture of peace and energy that we generate in those times of prayer. It might be only for a few minutes, but I do believe that we sow seeds in people's lives by that witness. Some of them ask if we'll pray for them.

What I do know is that they feel the impact of our music. They've never heard voices quite like ours, and they've never seen the intensity and passion we bring to our music. That's what makes them turn to us when they want to record an album, because they want to get that vibe into their recording. Quite soon we had so many requests from artists wanting backing singers, as well as companies wanting us to sing at corporate events, that we found ourselves effectively running a session agency. Occasionally we had to go out and find professional singers who could sing in our style, but wherever possible I used choir members, if they could get time off work or arrange to use some of their holiday allowance for weekday bookings. This was paid work, and since they were all giving their time to the choir on a voluntary basis, I thought they deserved to get something back where possible. In the early days we scarcely made enough money to cover the costs of transport, food and accommodation for a choir of around 100 members, let alone pay anyone.

We also started touring in Europe, invited by promoters who knew that we would be as big a draw in France, Spain and Germany as we were in the UK. It was another new experience for our young members, many of whom had never been abroad before, and had to get a passport for the first time. Andrea was an important member of the choir, and although we had a young family, we couldn't spare her. So we took the children on the road with us, and they played (and sang along) in the tour bus. In 1986 Lasse Olssen set up our first tour in Sweden – we always say that he cut his promotional teeth on LCGC: he is now one of the biggest rock promoters in Scandinavia. As usual with such a large group, it was the travel which was the most expensive item. The 90 choir members paid £75 each so that we could charter our own aircraft, but after paying for two coaches and all our food, there was no money left for hotels; we slept on the floor in classrooms and church halls. On the Sunday we arrived we attended a church service, but of course, as it was all in Swedish, no one could understand a word. The choir were so tired that they were dozing off in the pews, and I kept having to nudge them to keep them awake.

However, as we drove across country to concert halls and churches, their natural ebullience reasserted itself: we rehearsed as we travelled, singing and talking and laughing all the way. Two members, Dale Prime and Emil McKenzie, set up a mike at the front of the bus and proceeded to start "Radio LCGC", a hilarious continuous commentary on the tour. These two later went on to become the stand-up comedians Jefferson and Whitfield, combining jokes with reggae-style musical parody on the comedy circuit in places like Jongleurs, The Comedy Store and Comedy Café. They also wrote two all-black family pantomimes called *Yo, Cinders, Can You Butterfly?* and *Da Wiz*, which were hugely popular and played at the Hackney Empire and the Shepherd's Bush Theatre. That was the kind of talent we were nurturing.

In the same year, at the height of the Troubles in Northern Ireland, we played a concert called "Sing Out" at the Ulster Hall, Belfast. We were staying at the Europa Hotel, the most bombed building in the city. Nowadays we have become used to security checks at airports and public buildings, but in those days it was unheard of in England to have anyone stop you in the foyer of a building and check your bags. When we arrived at the concert hall we were amazed to find that a hut had been erected outside the door, acting as a sort of airlock for processing everyone who went in. We had to open our bags and empty our pockets: with drums and guitar cases as well as the ladies' handbags and all our costumes, it took a surprisingly long time.

Our first tour in Poland was also an eye-opener. In those days Poland was still a communist country, but a trickle of Western artists had begun touring the Eastern Bloc, and we had made contact with a budding new promoter called Marek Spendowski. We shared the tour with an American Gospel artist called Steve Taylor, and we had planned five shows.

The first one went well, but by the second one, word had reached the authorities – though whether they objected to the interactive style of our presentation, or the Christian sentiments we expressed, we never found out. We were performing in a huge building constructed by Hitler's armies, a brutal arrangement of concrete columns, so it wasn't a beautiful environment.

During the sound check we noticed that soldiers had begun to turn up and hang around outside, and when the concert began, they came in with the audience. We still didn't think anything of it, until the point where we taught the audience the song "Perfect Harmony" – which was our theme song at the time – and invited them to join hands and sing with us. The soldiers moved in among the seats and pushed people's hands down, forbidding them to stand up and take part in what was, after all, a demonstration of unity and community.

We sang on, but their leader then went to Marek and told him that the concert had to stop: this kind of demonstration (the audience were clapping, cheering and standing up together) was not allowed. No further concerts went ahead; we were made to surrender our passports; Marek was taken to the local army headquarters and held there; and we were escorted to the airport, handed our passports and told to leave.

We contacted the British Embassy in Warsaw (and Steve contacted the US Embassy, too) to protest about our treatment; they told us that Marek had been arrested and imprisoned for promoting "anti-government propaganda and Christianity".

He spent two years in prison, and we never expected to see him again.

However, some years later, after the collapse of communism, we were invited to perform in Warsaw by the British Council. The head of the Council came backstage to thank us for our performance, and said that he had brought along a special guest. The choir was gathering for a reception in the Green Room when in walked Marek and his family. There were tears and hugs as he introduced his wife and children. Some of the choir members were quite bemused, because they had joined only recently, and had no idea how concerned we had been about our part in Marek's troubles.

We were delighted to hear that he had flourished since his release: he is now one of the biggest promoters in Europe, and when he comes to the UK (for meetings of the International Music Managers Forum) we always meet up.

In 1984 we realized that the choir's ministry was taking up more hours than there were left after I'd done a day's work. In an enormous leap of faith both Lawrence Johnson and I left our jobs and committed ourselves to running the choir full time. It was a difficult time: with very little money coming in, we depended on state benefits to help us make ends meet. We had no carpets and Vernetta did all her crawling on bare floorboards. Andrea took some agency nursing work from time to time, though we both felt it was important for the children's security and development that she was a full-time mum. However, when she signed up to that, she hadn't expected to be answering phones, taking bookings and arranging tours at the same time!

The choir consisted of a large number of young people in their teens and early twenties, who regarded us as something between their youth leaders and their employers. We lived on a busy road and it seemed that everyone rang our doorbell as they went past, calling in for coffee, or a chat about the choir, or a prayer meeting.

Andrea would be trying to breastfeed and constantly getting up to answer the door or the phone. As our home was also the office, people came for planning meetings (more food and coffee), and since most of our members were young, they were always hungry, so they helped themselves from the fridge. God was good and we never starved, but we sometimes felt that the ministry was taking over our lives.

When Stephanie was born, Andrea's mum came to help with the new baby, and she was amazed at the way we were living. Quite apart from anything else, she felt that the children were over-stimulated by the constant comings and goings in the house. She suggested that we should keep our home separate from the office. It was good advice, and we moved to a town house in Highams Park. It was a cul-de-sac, so as the children grew they could play safely in the street with their friends, and best of all, the business meetings and endless phone calls could be diverted to the office. Off the beaten track, we had fewer unexpected visitors, too, so life became a little quieter for the family.

We managed to staff the office with volunteers at first, and because everyone was so enthusiastic and inspired by the way the choir was taking off, there was no shortage of offers – though managing the volunteers also took a great deal of organizing!

All in all, those first years of the choir's life were astonishing to all of us. What had started out as such a simple idea seemed to have blossomed into something unimaginable. We developed a national and then an international reputation almost from the start, playing with the biggest names in the business. From a church-based choir we had entered the mainstream entertainment business – something none of us had expected.

Recently Jenny LaTouche, our archivist (and the niece of the legendary Anton LaTouche), unearthed an old folder from 1986 which listed the choir's achievements in the first four years of its life. It's dazzling to see how rapidly we had risen to fame:

1983

Concerts

Mighty Clouds of Joy – Dominion Theatre, London

International Rock Gospel Concert – Wembley Conference Centre, London

A Time For All – Queen Elizabeth Hall, London

Television

Black on Black, Christmas Concert filmed at Kensington Temple – Channel 4

Radio

A Time for All from the Queen Elizabeth Hall – Radio London

Recording

"Fill My Cup" – single – Island Records

1984

Concerts

Gospel Joy – Riverside Studios, London

GLC Spring Festival – Jubilee Gardens, South Bank, London

Greenwich Festival – Greenwich Borough Hall, London

Mission to London – Queens Park Stadium, London

Afro-West-Indian Pentecostal Youth Celebration – Westminster Central Hall

Capital Music Festival with Al Green – Royal Albert Hall, London

Young, Gifted and Black – Shaw Theatre, London

Clark Sisters in Concert – Dominion Theatre, London

New Designers Fashion Show – Olympia, Earls Court, London

Television

We Gonna Sing, Gospel music documentary on LCGC – Channel 4

Sixty Minutes – BBC TV

Songs of Praise – BBC TV

Sunday Sunday – ITV

Saturday Superstore – BBC TV

Ebony – BBC TV

Rock Gospel Show, Christmas Special – BBC TV

TV-am – ITV

London Plus – BBC TV

Radio

In Concert from St Paul's, Finchley – Radio 2

Capital Radio Gospel Festival – Capital Radio

In Concert from The Studio, Streatham – Radio 1

Celebration of Christmas with Cliff Richard, Dana and Roy Castle, from the Fairfield Halls, Croydon – Radio 2

1985

Concerts

King George V Anniversary – St Paul's Cathedral, London, in the presence of the Royal Family

Capital Music Gospel Festival with James Cleveland – Royal Albert Hall, London

Guest appearance with Foreigner – Wembley Arena, London

Fashion for Famine – Grosvenor House Hotel, London

In Concert – Haymarket Theatre, London

Television

Songs of Praise – BBC TV

Wogan – BBC TV

Rock Gospel Show – BBC TV

Saturday Superstore – BBC TV

Pebble Mill at One – BBC TV

Royal Gala Performance in aid of the Commonwealth Games, recorded at the Playhouse Theatre, Edinburgh – BBC TV

Radio

Capital Radio Gospel Festival – Capital Radio

BBC Children in Need Appeal – Radio 2

Christmas Concert (one hour) on *Black Londoners* – Radio London

LCGC radio documentary – Radio London

When the Spirit Moves – Capital Radio

Gloria Hunniford Show – Radio 2

Oh, Isn't It Good, LCGC Good Friday programme – Radio 2

In Concert – *Feel the Spirit* programme – Radio 1

1986

Concerts

Gospel Meets Flamenco – Queen Elizabeth Hall, London

Caribbean Focus Concert with Casablanca Steel Band and the Metropolitan Police Band – Royal Albert Hall

Typhoo Music Festival – Liverpool Garden Site, Liverpool

Capital Music Gospel Festival (headlining) – Fairfield Halls, Croydon

Celebration of Christmas with Cliff Richard, Dana and Roy Castle – Wembley Conference Centre

Television

Sing Out – ten-part TV series featuring two LCGC concerts from the Ulster Hall, filmed in Ireland by Ulster TV

Royal Gospel Gala – in aid of the Save the Children Fund, at the Royal Albert Hall in the presence of HRH Princess Anne, for *Rock Gospel Show*, BBC TV

Rock Gospel Show – BBC TV

Fanfare for Elizabeth – 60th birthday celebrations for Her Majesty The Queen, recorded live at the Royal Opera House by ITV

Sunday Morning Worship from Rochester Cathedral – TVS

Club Mix – Channel 4

Radio

Janice Long Show – Radio 1

Good Morning Sunday – Radio 2

Caribbean Magazine – BBC World Service

Black Londoners – Radio London

Rice 'n' Peas – LBC

Radio Piccadilly

Radio Thamesmead

Recording

Feel the Spirit (live Swedish recording) – Cantio/Word

Over that period our style had been developing, alongside the maturity and confidence of our members. Back in 1983 we were very much a product of our church backgrounds. Even though the choir were bravely doing something outside church, they were influenced by the traditional expectations of their churches. In the case of the women, that meant a particular style of clothing: they performed the first concerts wearing a uniform of grey pleated dresses and little hats with a blue net veil at the front and a small bow at the back. Although Andrea and I pleaded with them to wear stage make-up, the idea was very shocking to them. One or two of the girls began to have some idea of how unforgiving stage lighting could be, and made small concessions: a favourite was "Transparent Burgundy®" lipstick – nowadays you would probably describe it as lip gloss. I think they knew they had burnt their boats as far as the church was concerned at that point! Fortunately, over time the church position has relaxed, and very few Pentecostal churches frown on make-up today.

It was a long while before any of the women wore trousers, though we began to get sponsorship to help with our wardrobe requirements. Someone negotiated a deal with a company called Aitch Knitwear, and for a while we had warm jumpers for travelling in, and yellow jackets and white skirts, trousers and tee-shirts. Mostly we wore simple colour combinations: white shirts with navy trousers or skirts. Nowadays we mostly wear our own clothes in matching colours: all black, or all white, or black and white. For a long while most people's idea of a Gospel choir was a group wearing church choir robes, like the American choirs they had seen on television. We didn't very often do that, mostly because of the expense, but we do have some robes now, which we wear if requested – generally for weddings.

Choreography is another thing which has moved on over the years. Lawrence Johnson was especially good at that, though when we look back at old recordings we seem pretty static compared to our energetic routines today. Back then we would maybe do some clapping from side to side, or shift from foot to foot in time to the music, but most other choirs (like the COGIC choir) simply stood still, so moving at all was fairly revolutionary. It was part of making our singing a performance as well as an act of worship, part of the move towards entertainment that we were involved in, and it also had the effect of making our audiences want to stand up and join in!

The choreography is led by the choir director, who conducts and leads from the front and indicates when he or she wants the choir to move. Over the years we've had some fantastic leaders. When Lawrence Johnson moved on (he later formed Nu Colours and had a hit with "Special Kinda Lover" in the 1990s) he was followed by Peter Francis, Orville Thomas, and later on Daniel Thomas, who stepped in while I spent six months away from the choir, directing *Mama I Want to Sing* in the West End. Daniel directed with flair and creativity: he had the gift of getting the best out of the choir, keeping eye contact with them and telling a story with his hands at the same time.

Every director has their own style, and the choreography changes with each of them. Wendi Rose took movement to a new level – when she started with us the choir complained (only half seriously) that it was Gospel gymnastics! She didn't rehearse the moves, she just stood in front and danced at them, and expected them to follow after a couple of passes. They never knew what to expect, and hoped they'd be able to keep up with her inspiration as it came. (Wendi now works as a full-time session singer, providing the backing for groups like Blur, Spiritualized and Gorillaz.) Our latest acquisition is Rebecca Thomas, who is bringing her own style to the choir.

It's always been our policy to duplicate all the key positions, like choir directors, so that we are able to send groups to two different events at the same time, and we are never left short of leaders in cases of illness or unexpected diary clashes. Stephanie is the youngest choir director we ever had – she was leading at the age of thirteen! Vernetta was a little older when she first took to the stage. Both girls helped to conduct and to arrange songs, and they had a big input into the choir's repertoire. Leonn is the choir's drummer but he also sings and conducts.

Having a choir where everyone is an accomplished musician means that we have enormous flexibility in how we use our singers. Because we aren't singing from printed music we aren't tied to a single version. So in rehearsal I could pick out any singer and ask them to come out and give us their interpretation of a song – the "call and response" or "lead singer and choir backing" format, however you like to think of it, means that the flexibility is in-built. Every singer sounds different, and when they're leading, each person can improvise their own embellishments around the core line of the music. It's a bit like a jazz improvisation – as long as you come back to the chord you're aiming for, you can take the music where you want. That's what makes Gospel music so creative and spontaneous: the song is still there at the heart of it, but every performance is unique to the singer taking the lead, so it's always fresh and exciting.

CHAPTER 8

Keep moving

In the early days of the choir we were a large group of almost 100 – too large for some stages, and expensive and unwieldy to move around. Just paying for food and accommodation used up most of the fees we were earning, and we needed two coaches to take us and the band and instruments anywhere. Of course, the way we formed the choir related to its original purpose: we wanted to gather talented young musicians from different churches, train them, and send them back to disseminate what they'd learned among the wider church community. Consequently we had never held auditions; Lawrence and I would visit church choirs and bands and invite people whose sound we liked to come and join us.

This method produced a team of singers who were full of enthusiasm but of mixed abilities. As our bookings rolled in we were beginning to realize that God's plans for us were bigger and more exciting than we had ever dreamed. We were moving out from the churches and into the wider world, which had always been my aim: I wanted to do something other than preach to the converted. Music conveys a message beyond words, it goes straight to the heart, and I knew that by singing with all our heart and soul we convinced people that our faith was real and had something to say to them. But the world of entertainment which we had entered was also a business. People were paying to hear us, or paying for groups of session singers, and that meant we had to aim for excellence. There was no scope for saying that the sound wasn't quite right because we were amateurs. We had to raise our game.

Unfortunately, what that meant in the short term was that the choir had to be slimmed down. We needed to keep a core of about fifty of our best singers, and the only way to do that was to put everyone through an audition process. It was traumatic for the choir, who had bonded over four years of travelling, rehearsing and singing together, and it was painful for the leaders who had to conduct the auditions and the sometimes difficult interviews that followed, but it had to be done.

We now have a choir which varies between forty and fifty members; our average performing group is around twelve singers plus the band. We are a mixture of professional musicians (who sing or play in other groups as well, for a living) and volunteers who are students or have other jobs. What all our members have in common is their faith. Some have church membership, others don't, but they are all believers: if asked, any one of them would be able to give their testimony, and tell how they came to faith in the Lord Jesus Christ.

We have to be very selective, because lots of non-Christians are good singers who would love to sing with us, but they aren't the people I want. I have always been convinced that to sing Gospel music effectively you have to believe what you're singing. If you don't have that faith, you aren't singing from the heart: it just becomes words sung to a tune, and you don't have the passion to convey the love, or the repentance, or the joy you feel. That makes it a no-go area for non-Christians.

The choir members feel the same. Yvonne White says: "When I first joined LCGC I didn't know we were doing anything groundbreaking, I didn't realize we were paving the way for a new acceptance and enthusiasm for Gospel music. I just enjoyed singing about my faith. I couldn't believe that I was being given the opportunity to sing about the Lord I love, the chance to reach so many people who don't believe. The best thing was that for the first time in my life I felt that I was truly fulfilling the Great Commission of Jesus Christ in Matthew 28:19, when he said to his disciples, 'Therefore go and make disciples of all nations, baptising them in the name of the Father and of the Son and of the Holy Spirit, and teaching them to obey everything I have commanded you. And surely I am with you always, to the very end of the age.' It was such a privilege."

Our faith was profoundly challenged on one of our early tours. We were travelling through Norway late at night in freezing conditions. Our regular driver, Dave Sorkin, had recently bought a new coach, so most of the choir were enjoying the comfort of the new seats and catching up on some sleep. I was in my usual seat just behind the driver, but the night was pitch black and the road wasn't lit, so I couldn't see beyond the beam of our headlights. We had been climbing up a mountain road for a long while, and at last we came over the brow of the hill, only to find that the road was covered in black ice. Dave touched the brakes and the coach immediately went into an uncontrollable skid. We were veering wildly across the road as he fought to gain control, and the choir were woken by him shouting "I can't stop it!"

Suddenly I saw headlights coming towards us, but there was nothing Dave could do to avoid a collision. For a moment I thought that the car had passed us safely, but then there was a sickening crash as it struck our side near the rear of the coach. The blow swung us further across the road, and we slid sideways and came to a standstill against a roadside barrier. When I looked out, I could see that beyond the barrier, there was a sheer drop of hundreds of feet: if we hadn't been slowed by the impact, we would certainly have shot over the edge into the ravine.

Dave jumped out and ran back to the car, and I and a few choir members followed him. We stopped when he turned and came back towards us with his head in his hands, crying, "I've killed a baby." A couple of our members who were nurses ran on to try to help. When they looked in the car they saw a woman and a child, injured but alive; what Dave had seen on the back seat was the driver's head.

Everyone was stunned and horrified. Then, in the apparently empty darkness, lights began to come on – there were houses on the other side of the road, and people had heard the crash. They started arriving with blankets, called the emergency services, and took the choir members into their homes and gave them food and drink.

Eventually another coach came and took us on to our destination, and we had to take stock. Dave was in a terrible state, and we decided that he would have to fly home. He didn't drive again for many years; that crash was the end of his one-man company. The choir had commitments in Norway, and although no one wanted to go on after what had happened, we knew we couldn't let people down.

It was a moment when we really had to lean on our faith. We recognized that God had spared our lives, but we were devastated by the death of the other driver. How could we cope? Only by going on to our next concert in Trondheim. There were many tears in the concert that followed. We explained to the audience what had happened, and we wept and prayed together, and there was a real bond between the choir and the audience that night.

The crash brought the choir together on a different level. We were accustomed to the sense of unity that came from the adrenalin rush of dancing and singing together, but now we faced the dark side of our shared experience. We had been in the presence of death, and we shared our feelings of shock, guilt and anguish. All we could do was to hold on to each other and our Lord, and try to express our sorrow and thanksgiving to God.

It was on another Scandinavian tour in 1986 that we produced our first album, *Feel the Spirit*, which was planned as an important element of our agent's promotion strategy. It was recorded live in Sweden, with a mobile recording unit stationed outside the church where we were performing. By 10 p.m. (the usual Swedish start time) the place was packed, and they were turning people away outside. The fantastic reception, combined with the fact that we knew everything was being recorded, encouraged us to give it everything we had. We sang, we clapped, we danced, and we put our whole souls into it. It was midnight before we staggered off stage, sweating and exhausted, but knowing we had given the performance of our lives. The audience was wildly enthusiastic and the applause was still dying down as people gathered their belongings ready to leave. The choir were all collapsing onto chairs backstage and kicking off their shoes when Lasse Ollsen, our agent, called Lawrence and me out of the room. A very shamefaced recording engineer came to meet us. Something had gone wrong: nothing had been recorded.

We stared at one another in dismay: I knew how much it had cost to get the choir over there in the first place. Lasse wanted passionately to promote us in Sweden, but recording this concert was the key to financing the tour.

"Bazil, we can do nothing without this recording," he said. "Can you get the choir to go back on stage and do the whole thing again for the microphones?"

It was a tall order. I knew how exhausted the choir members were – but I knew we had to honour our agreement with Lasse. Somehow Lawrence and I had to find the words to persuade them not just to haul themselves to their feet, but to deliver a second performance as good as the first – without an audience. Was there any point? There was no chance we could recapture the atmosphere of a live show at 1 a.m. in an empty church.

Lasse got someone to hurry out to the front to see if any audience members were still around hoping for an encore. Meanwhile, we did the only thing we could think of – we called the choir to prayer, which is always the heart of what we do. That's why it's so important to have a choir which is made up of believers. We prayed for God's power to unite our hearts and minds, and asked him to help us to dig deeper to find the reserves of energy that would enable us to accomplish what we set out to do. Lasse returned as we were finishing our prayer, and smiled at me. I thought he had caught some of the energy that was coming back to us.

We made our way wearily back towards the stage, and stopped in amazement. I realized why Lasse was smiling: the entire audience were still in their seats! Hearing that we were repeating the show, they had stayed to hear the whole concert again. And bless them, they clapped and cheered and shouted just as much the second time round, urging us on to give a second performance almost as good as the first.

Feel the Spirit (on the Myrrh label) wasn't our first recording: earlier that year we had recorded the single "Fill My Cup" (written by our own Howard Francis) at Island Records. Other albums followed: *Gospel Greats* on EMI in 1990; *Hush and Listen* for Kingsway Music in 1992; and *Live! Inspiration & Power* for One Voice Records in 1996. Then there were a string of recordings on the FAR label: *Out of Many, One Voice* in 1998; *Joy to the World* in 1999; *Force Behind the Power* in 2001; *Negro Spirituals and Gospel Songs* in 2002; our *21st Anniversary Concert, Live at Abbey Road* in 2003; *Keep Moving* (limited edition) in 2007; and most recently, on BMG, *Glorious* in 2010.

Gospel Greats was another memorable recording. We'd been asked to put together an album of hymns and Gospel songs, so four of us – Lawrence Johnson, Howard Francis, Wayne Wilson and myself – got together and put the LCGC stamp on them with our spicier rearrangements. We rehearsed the choir and took them down to a church in Finchley which had been hired by the producer, Gordon

Lorenz.[17] When we got there we realized that the balance was all wrong; the drums were dominating everything, but there was no cubicle to enclose the drum kit. In the end we improvised: we built a box out of old mattresses and put our drummer, Nicky Brown, inside. He recorded the whole album from inside this fortress, with just a peep-hole so he could see the conductor. We put the whole album down in about three evenings, and everyone would come down to Finchley straight from work to do it.

One of my favourite recordings ever is our *21st Anniversary Concert* – it was special for so many reasons. For a start, there was the fact that the choir had gone on for so long, doing new things and growing and developing all that time. We'd come such a long way. We had recorded at Abbey Road before, in some of the smaller studios, but we'd never been in Studio 1. There was so much anticipation in the air as the sound guys were setting up and the TV crew filming the DVD were checking the lighting and camera angles. Then everyone came in and we took time to pray as a choir, committing the whole thing to God. People talked about how they felt about being there, their hopes for the project, and how we were turning the whole studio into a church for one night. It certainly felt like church – we were going to worship God. Whatever that studio had been used for before, for that one night it was dedicated to God, and we used it to lift up the name of Jesus. It really brought the whole thing home to me, what we'd done in taking our music out of the churches and into the world. Some people disapprove of the whole rock scene, and call it the enemy's territory, but we were taking it over for God. That was a very powerful feeling.

The other special thing about it was the guest artists who recorded with us. We had called on various friends to join our celebration, and one of them was Sam Moore. Sam was a huge soul star in the 1960s, and as a youngster I'd listened to his hits like "Soul Man" and "Hold on I'm Coming". He chose to sing an old traditional song called "In the Garden", and when we were rehearsing he told me how much that song meant to him. "It reminds me of the church where I first learned to sing," he said, "and how special God has been to me, protecting me all these years." Other guests were Paul Carrack, Martin Smith and Matt Redman. Matt's singing of "Blessed Be Your Name" ushered in a powerful sense of worship that was a blessing to all of us.

Our latest album is *Glorious*, and this was another new departure for us. Previous albums had showcased our fantastic musicians: now we wanted to bring our vocal skills to the fore with more *a cappella* work. We were aiming to reach a new market, the people who prefer middle-of-the-road sounds like The Priests, so we dipped into rock and pop territory, covering songs like "Let it be" and "Hallelujah" alongside inspirational anthems like "Abide with Me" and "Amazing Grace", and the Gospel classics "Glory, Glory, Hallelujah" and "Down in the River to Pray".

Of course, when we're working with other artists to provide backing singers, whether for recordings or live performances, the dynamic is a little different: God isn't central to what they do. We don't have a problem with this: it's an issue that has been around ever since the first American Gospel singers came out of the church in the 1920s and started working in jazz and blues clubs, or even just performing in ordinary concert halls. Gospel music isn't an industry, in the sense that there are no full-time Gospel groups making their living in venues which promote Gospel music, and Gospel albums don't sell enough units and thus generate enough income to provide employment for the musicians involved.

The first payment received by the choir was from a youth organization in Hoxton, who had a government grant to provide music facilities for unemployed youngsters. They came to us and asked if some of our musicians and song-writers would run workshops, which we did. The payment was small, but it enabled a few of our members to see that they had the potential to find work as professional musicians. I began to have a vision for a full-time Gospel choir, with enough bookings to enable me to pay them properly – but I eventually realized that there wasn't enough work for that to happen. What we have ended up with is a pool of about forty members, many of whom are professional musicians, but they are all freelances: they spend some of their time with the choir, and make up their income with other jobs in the music industry, as session singers, songwriters or soloists; others have other jobs or work in our own office supporting the administration side.

Having this number of singers to call on means that if a client calls from Spain with a booking, we can put together a team (such as twelve singers, five musicians and a technician) and negotiate a fee that will allow us to pay an appropriate salary to each member. The same system applies to our popular service of music for weddings, corporate events, and other bookings. Often several events will be going on at the same time, so our administration team have to be highly organized.

Running the choir as a business doesn't deflect us from our core belief that our music is a witness, and that our lives, our fellowship and the central place we give to prayer and trust in our Lord can work alongside the lyrics of the Gospel songs to demonstrate this. Like those early Gospel singers, we sometimes meet with disapproval from the churches, especially when we sing with artists whose material is not primarily Gospel. We have recorded a version of "Hey Ya!" with Razorlight (the B side of a single called "Vice"[18]); we have sung with Will Young (on his album *From Now On*[19]), Blur ("Tender"[20]), Erasure (*Erasure*[21]), Nick Cave and the Bad Seeds (the double album *Abattoir Blues/The Lyre of Orpheus*[22]), Gorillaz (*Demon Days*[23]), and also Paul McCartney, Elton John, Westlife, Tori Amos and Madonna.

One of our most memorable jobs was with Luther Vandross in 1994. He is rightly held in high esteem throughout the world for his beautiful voice and amazing vocal ability. The usual rehearsal time with an artist is one or two days, but we worked together for about two weeks, rehearsing on a set erected in the Docklands Arena, which was later moved to the Royal Albert Hall.

The impressive thing was that Luther didn't leave the teaching of the songs to his musical director, but taught the choir himself, using his own backing group to demonstrate them. He befriended the choir and endeared himself to them because he took so much care over getting the balance right: the end result was a fantastic blend of voices. At the actual performance, accompanied by the Royal Philharmonic Orchestra, we felt as if we'd been working together for years.

Most unusually, when Luther himself spoke to the audience he acknowledged the choir's (and my) contribution: an example of his generous spirit. He left a fantastic impression of a warm human being as well as a performer.

In 1997 I had a break from conducting the choir. Vy Higginsen was the writer, producer and director of *Mama, I Want to Sing*, the longest-running off-Broadway musical in the history of American theatre. She was bringing the show to the UK, and wanted to recruit British singers and musicians. The choir alone was not a big enough pool of talent, so I brought together artists from all over the country, together with a few locals from London. I thought I'd like to go with them and meet the management company, so I went along to the auditions. The American musical director, Wesley Naylor, was there, and he asked me if I would accompany one of the soloists, which I did. Wesley liked my style of playing and thought I would be right for the show – though I had no intention of auditioning myself. I saw my role just as that of "fixer", finding people to sing and play. I was amazed to be offered the position of musical director.

This gave me all sorts of problems – I told them that my time was fully occupied running my own choir, but Wesley was very persuasive. He encouraged me to bring in a substitute director for the choir (Daniel Thomas stood in for me, and did it extremely well) and to delegate other duties to the office. By this time things were running very smoothly, so I agreed that it would be an exciting new experience to be involved in a big West End production.

The musical tells the story of Doris Troy (Vy Higginsen's sister), a girl from a Pentecostal church who becomes a singing star. In the original US production, Vy's brother Randy Higginsen played the role of their father, Revd Randolph Higginsen, and Doris Troy herself played the role of their mother, Geraldine. I was astonished when I attended the first rehearsal and realized that the leading role was being played by Chaka Khan. In time she was followed by Denise Williams; then Sharon D. Clarke and Mica Paris took the title role one after the other. I had never expected to be directing stars as big as these.

The show was a big event for the Pentecostal church – every night you would see ladies in hats in the audience, church members who would never have attended a theatre if it were not for the subject-matter – and also for the black community. The great music and star performers drew in big audiences, and they were mixed, black and white. For the first time some black people realized that it could be OK to go to the theatre, and for the first time some white people got a glimpse of black church life. The big names drew in others, too: when American artists were touring the UK they came to see the show, and every night some star or other was invited up from the audience to the stage to take a round of applause: Stevie Wonder, Prince, and Luther Vandross, among others. When Luther came up on stage he looked down and spotted me in the orchestra pit, and called out, "Hey, Baz, how ya doin' there?"

Stephanie must have seen the show about fourteen times. She wasn't allowed to come on school nights, but she often came to the Saturday matinees, and went backstage to meet the cast – she was one star-struck little girl!

It was on the back of *Mama* that LCGC got its entry into Japan. One of the show's sponsors was a Mr Shibaoka, and he invited Doris Troy to do some concerts in Japan. Doris needed backing vocalists and musicians, so we put together a package of six vocalists, a drummer, bass and keyboard, all from LCGC, with Doris as the star and lead singer. The tour went very well, but Doris was getting older, and when she was no longer fit enough to travel, LCGC went on doing the concerts alone. We remained friends, and even when Doris gave up touring and retired to live in Las Vegas, she often used to call me to see what the choir was up to.

What the choir was "up to" was mostly a lot of hard work, but the members found time to relax and socialize together, too. It wasn't long before romance was in the air, and several couples fell in love and married while they were with us. Patricia Knight (a LROR founder member) was one of our star soloists, with a beautiful soprano voice. We were thrilled when she married John Scott, our sound engineer. John's nickname was The General because he was so stern: if he told you to be quiet during a sound check, you did just that. Other choir weddings included Wayne Wilson (who played keyboard and wrote some of our songs) and Patricia Nelson; Peter Francis (who took over as choir director when Lawrence Johnson left us) and Paula Lamonious; Michael Smith and Angela Lamonious; Eion Marche and Debbie Maynard; and Dale Prime (half of Jefferson and Whitfield) and Sharon Simpson.

Life for the choir never stands still – we really do "keep moving". As well as our own concerts, recordings and tours, over the years we have been invited to sing at all kinds of events – the 2009 Cup Final at Wembley, for instance. That was a first for us and a massive deal for the choir – you can hardly have a more high-profile performance than singing for the crowd at Wembley and the millions watching on TV around the world. It took a year to set up: Rick Beasley arranged for us to record "Abide with Me" as a single, which he sent to ITV with a view to convincing them to break with tradition and replace the usual classical singer with a choir to lead the singing before the kick-off. The build-up before the game was fantastic, and the response from the crowd in the stadium was amazing.

Some events are simply professional engagements, but others are closer to our hearts. One of our most moving performances was in the early 1990s, after Nelson Mandela was released from his long imprisonment in South Africa. On his first visit to the UK after his release, hosted by Prince Charles, he came to the Brixton Leisure Centre, and we were asked to perform the African National Anthem, "Nkosi Sikele Afrika". The anthem embodies Mandela's vision of the "rainbow nation", with all the races working together, as the lyrics include five of the most widely spoken languages: Xhosa, Zulu, Sethoto, Afrikaans and English. It was especially meaningful for us because that vision is very close to our own aspirations. Our choir includes both black and white singers, and we hope that our music brings people together.

Most moving, perhaps, was the concert we gave in aid of my own home country, Montserrat. My home villages were in the foothills of the Soufrière Hills, and when I was a child I remember that if the wind was in the right direction you would sometimes catch the sour smell of sulphur. There had been occasional earth tremors long ago, but no one worried about it: the volcano hadn't been active since the seventeenth century. When I went back to Montserrat as an adult, I went on a tourist trip to see it, and stood in a group looking down into the crater. I never dreamed that it would ever erupt.

In July 1995 I heard on the television news that the volcano seemed to be active again: Plymouth and many other settlements had been evacuated. It was alarming but it sounded as though the authorities were monitoring the activity, and had the situation under control. A few weeks later there was a major eruption, and a pyroclastic flow (a mixture of gas, volcanic ash and rock) had covered the city in debris several metres deep. Once again I made a few calls and checked that family members were OK, and then forgot about it. I assumed that the activity would subside; I had lived all my early years on the side of the volcano, so somehow I didn't take it too seriously.

It seemed that some of the locals took it too lightly, as well. They were on the spot, so they knew that there were regular minor eruptions, but evacuation made life too difficult for them. They were farmers, and they made their living from the land – Montserrat has no industry and very few shops. They had animals to care for, and everything they owned was in the tiny houses they had been persuaded to leave. So gradually they began to drift back, and went back to farming as they had always done.

Then, in June 1997, completely without warning, the volcano erupted again. A flow reached Plymouth, to the south-west, but at the same time, the other side of the dome collapsed, sending another flow eastwards down the Tar River Valley towards the little villages of Tuitts (where I lived with my mother), Farms (where Errol and I lived with my father) and Bethel (where we went to school). Pyroclastic flow moves incredibly fast – up to 450 m.p.h. – so no one in the path of the rock, ash and lethal gas had a chance. Nineteen people lost their lives.

When you look at a satellite picture of Montserrat today, almost the whole of the southern part of the island is a dull grey colour, covered in ash and rock. More than half the island is uninhabitable. Many of the surviving population left the island, but for those who were left, life was impossibly hard. The airport had been destroyed, and water and electricity supplies had been damaged.

One great supporter of Montserrat was Sir George Martin. His Air Studios in London had long been a mecca for recording artists, but in 1977 he visited Montserrat and fell in love with the place.

He built a sister studio, Air Studios Montserrat, which was visited by famous rock artists like Dire Straits, Duran Duran, Michael Jackson, Stevie Wonder, The Rolling Stones, and Eric Clapton. In 1989 the building was destroyed by Hurricane Hugo, but dozens of musicians had fond memories of the island.

Sir George organized a benefit concert at the Albert Hall, and LCGC was delighted to play a part. Throughout the concert my thoughts were with the beautiful island of my childhood, green and lush in my memory, and now sterile and grey. It was heartbreaking. Many of the choir have Caribbean contacts, and they all shared my feelings. We were joined in a simultaneous show on the island by the Montserrat artist Arrow, singing (with some irony) a soca number, "Feeling hot, hot, hot", and modern technology enabled us to exchange images of the two performances.

A few months later I took the choir to Montserrat to perform again, and this time I took my mother with us: she was thrilled to be returning to the island, but like all of us, she was sobered by the scale of the devastation. It was an emotional day.

Another amazing experience was in 2007 when the British Council held a commemorative event in Ghana to celebrate the 200th anniversary of the British Act of Parliament that abolished the slave trade. It was held at Elmina Castle, the first European slave-trading post in sub-Saharan Africa. It was here that the slaves were held in dungeons before being forcibly transported overseas. LCGC had been invited to sing in the ceremony, demonstrating a spirit of unity between the Africans and us, a choir mainly formed of the descendants of slaves. We joined with Ghana's Winneba Youth Choir to sing "When the Saints Come Marching In".

It was incredibly moving, and I wept when I looked at the cells where so many thousands of our forefathers were chained. It reminded me how important it is that we shouldn't forget our origins. Black Britons may be born in the UK but they have their own cultural history, and they need to know about their roots, going back to the plantations and before that to Africa. It was a moment that brought me full circle, back to my childhood in Montserrat, working in the cotton fields, and to the music which has become my life, with its echoes of the African drums and dances, the slave songs, and the hope of the Gospel.

CHAPTER 9

My soul says yes

The choir's ministry was never just about sharing our faith through singing. As Christians we always wanted to live out our faith as well as sing about it. As soon as LCGC was established those of us leading the choir (Lawrence Johnson, Delroy Powell and I) became aware of the responsibility we had shouldered. By the end of 1983 we had over 100 young people in our care, drawn from various churches. Rehearsing, travelling to concerts and performing all took up a lot of time – time they would usually be spending within their own home churches. Fortunately we had all been choir directors and youth leaders in our own churches, so we understood our task: to encourage, teach, nurture and disciple our young people.

LCGC had become a community in itself, and our youngsters gained a huge amount from their membership – the opportunity to sing, play instruments, and improve their musical skills and pass them on to others. The choir had its own social life, running a football team that competed locally and even holding its own sports days. The first of these was held at Finsbury Park and included not only serious athletics events but also egg-and-spoon and three-legged races for the less sporting members. It finished with a pool party at a local leisure centre.

Like any church youth group, we organized residential "retreat" weekends which combined fun with music and Bible study, but of course our young people also had the advantage of travelling together throughout Great Britain and Europe, and later, around the world.

From 1986 onwards Andrea and Cheryl Mead (the publicity team) wrote, edited and printed the LCGC magazine, which we called *On the Rock*. This featured cartoons and jokes alongside "Speaker's Corner" (a reflection on a Bible passage), that month's birthdays, the forthcoming month's calendar of bookings, prayer requests, and accounts of what was going on in all areas of the choir's life. One popular feature was called "Live Issues", in which members raised questions which troubled them in their spiritual lives, and older Christians attempted to answer. These were nothing if not frank and honest: in the debate about relationships between Christians and non-Christians, one young man complained: "'Seek ye first' doesn't keep your bed warm at night."

During tours, each day a different choir member would write up a diary account of events, to be published in the following month's *Rock* so that those left at home could share in the experience.

On the Rock also featured letters of appreciation from schoolchildren ("I really felt part of the singing and that's why I was singing so LOUD"), churches ("The Messiah's Heralds wish to congratulate you on winning the Commonwealth Institute Caribbean Focus Award for Community Involvement") and even coach drivers ("Thank you and your team for the wonderful time we had driving you around the schools of Bournemouth... for making us a part of what [you] were teaching the children").

The monthly calendar indicated how busy we were, and also the range of community activities we were involved in: in one month we gave performances in London, Southampton and Cardiff, led workshops in churches and schools, took part in worship in a cathedral, and visited hospitals and prisons.

The hospital and prison work was all done on a charitable basis, supported mainly by our commercial work; we also visited children's homes and other care organizations. In her report for *On the Rock* Primrose Bartley wrote:

The afternoon was very enjoyable, we sang songs such as "Perfect Harmony", "Nobody Knows", "Swing Low" and "My Soul Says Yes". The audience of about 60 included approximately 20 elderly people, they responded quietly, but you could see the joy on their faces. Joanne and Corinne gave testimonies about how they found life as Christians. Any doubts I may have had about the future organisation of hospital visits went as we chatted to the audience at the end. Many of them said it was the best afternoon singing they had heard for a long time and I will never forget a small Trinidadian lady who had had two legs amputated, yet still sat through every song clapping and singing along. She told me she felt the Lord touching her as we sang and wished we could have sung the song "Somebody touched me, touched my soul"... I know it's important for us to be in church on a Sunday, but remember those we're singing to can't be in God's house, so we should be bringing the service to them.

The prisons work came about because the Governor of Rochester Prison was a Christian. He was very aware that a disproportionate number of young black men ended up in prison, and he thought that our singers would provide positive role models for them. This fitted well with the LCGC vision for community service, so we went and led a Sunday service for him. It was a transforming experience for our members. They were used to going along to church and sitting in the congregation; going into a prison as the ministers was exciting because it felt like putting their Christianity into practice. After that they were eager to take up the invitations that flooded in from other prisons.

The visits usually took the form of a mini-concert with an interval, in which choir members and inmates mingled and talked, sometimes exchanging addresses so they could write to each other. Many friendships arose, sometimes followed up by personal visits. One Christmas we were invited back to Rochester specially to help relieve the seasonal tension. On Christmas Day and Boxing Day most of the prison officers were on leave, so the prisoners were only allowed out of their cells for meals. This situation caused a great deal of frustration, so the choir were asked to go along to provide some Christmas cheer. Apparently just the fact that the guys knew we were coming helped to keep them settled.

We also visited the women's prison at Bullwood Hall, where we gave concerts and also had group discussions with the girls. Tony McKenzie wrote of one session:

The girls asked us the question, "Have you always been good?" meaning have any of you had hard times. The reply to this was "No!" From this turn in the tide we were able to witness. They enjoyed the session so much that we were asked to go back a second time to see the same girls.

Soon we were visiting several youth custody centres and prisons on a monthly basis: Feltham, Rochester and Huntercombe Youth Custody Centres, and Pentonville, Wormwood Scrubs, Holloway and Standford Hill Prisons.

Personal relationships became very important. Andrea met one young man known as "Ice" in Canterbury Prison. When she asked him about his nickname, he said it was because he had "cut" a prison guard: when he was angry he became violent in an icy, controlled way. He himself had a long scar across his face. Andrea offered to find him someone of his own age and culture to visit him, but he insisted that he wanted to talk to her. She visited him whenever he sent her a visiting order (all visits have to be pre-arranged) and occasionally she would receive a call from the prison when Ice was acting up, refusing to co-operate, and had to be locked in his cell. She would travel down to Canterbury to talk to him and calm him down.

In Wormwood Scrubs we met an older Caribbean man called Eric who became something of a father figure to the choir. Although he had a history of violent offences he was always very polite and gentle with us. He valued the friendships he made with the choir members, and tried to repay them by making gifts of jewellery boxes and plaques out of matchsticks. Eventually Eric gave his life to the Lord, and invited three members of the choir to witness his baptism in the prison chapel. The week before his baptism he wrote:

> *I am now really looking forward to Sunday and all credit goes to LCGC. I owed it all to you and the others because you all have accepted me as I am. Glory be to Jesus. I know that you all cared about me and have accepted me as a friend. I know too well that it is the work of Jesus so I have made up my mind to be grateful to him by accepting him as my personal Saviour… LCGC have broke that barrier which was holding me back for a very very long time.*

Sadly, Eric committed suicide just before his release – we wondered whether, after so long in prison, he was too afraid of life outside.

This gave us some understanding of just how difficult it is for some prisoners to manage the transition to the world outside – obviously getting back into normal life is a major factor in managing to "go straight" and avoiding the revolving door of prison, quite apart from what Eric may have suffered in fearing his release. Andrea decided that the obvious way to continue our prison work was to help offenders prepare for their release, and support them afterwards. Together with Claudette Brown and Primrose Bartley, she put together the plan for "The People's Place", a scheme offering care, rehabilitation and resettlement for ex-offenders of any race, colour or creed. Initially they wanted to provide it in any area of the UK, but eventually funding limitations meant they had to settle for helping those coming back into London.

The work started inside the prisons, through the prison education services, offering pre-release courses covering the life skills needed, including keeping out of trouble. Nowadays we wouldn't be allowed the freedom to do some of the things we did then. Once, Andrea was running a pre-release session called "Action and Reaction" in Aylesbury Prison – a course to help young men realize that they are responsible for their actions, that they can control their responses and they don't have to react with violence. However, such courses today don't employ the radical steps Andrea took. There was a young man called Bola whom she knew quite well. She went up to him and slapped his face: her point was made as everyone saw the expressions that crossed his face as he subdued his initial impulse to strike her back. She apologized immediately, explained her reasoning and led a discussion on impulsive behaviour. (Of course, what she did technically constituted an assault.) After his release, Bola was one of the young men who started coming to church.

Outside the prison, we worked with the Probation Service, helping prisoners to obtain accommodation and find jobs. We also operated a café and drop-in centre for ex-offenders, housed in the office building we leased at 13–21 Hoxton Street, which we called The London Gospel Centre. It was opened in January 1988 by our patron, HRH The Prince of Wales, Prince Charles. At first all those running The People's Place (as we called our prison work), and the choir members working alongside them, were working voluntarily; later we got more funding which allowed us to employ one or two administrative staff. Andrea was Chairperson of The People's Place, and she enjoyed helping to organize our prison and hospital work, as well as doing a hundred and one other things for the choir.

The People's Place project was closed in 1996, mainly because it got harder to get funding. Funding providers moved their money into preventative work in schools, hoping to keep youngsters out of trouble, and though we were still able to get grants for projects like the pre-release courses, we could not fund the core work of supporting the offices and the administration.

The whole operation had been run alongside the administration of the choir. The London Gospel Centre was the realization of our vision to set up a one-stop shop for everything to do with Gospel: help and advice; a source for artists wanting session musicians or backing singers, or schools wanting someone to lead workshops; and even equipment hire. Some of these activities had commercial potential which we could tap to cover the costs of our community work, so we could buy fuel for the ageing minibus which took us to prisons and hospitals where our members were doing so much wonderful work. The London Gospel Centre was set up as a workers' co-operative, with everyone taking a share of the work.

A crucial role was played by Maureen Ellis, the choir's first secretary. A legal secretary by profession, she had grown up under my tutelage in LROR. Now she gave up all her spare time to running the choir, using the considerable organizational skills she had acquired in her day job. She ran a tight ship: realizing that she couldn't run all the complex administration herself, she soon set up a team of secretaries feeding information to her from all the departments, including Merchandizing, The People's Place and Equipment Hire.

When we bought our own PA system for the choir we realized we could maximize its potential by hiring it out between concerts. We were learning to be entrepreneurial. The result was Dove Sounds (PA and Equipment Hire) which we launched in 1986 after trying it out at a few small events. This put further pressure on some of our hard-working members: John Scott, Mark Williams, Patrick Myers, Nigel Wilson and Joan Todd. Their average working day lasted about twenty hours: loading the van, driving to the venue, setting up, sound-checking, operating the system for the wedding, church event or concert, then taking everything down and driving home. They did this for at least three weekends a month and sometimes midweek as well, but their efforts were very worthwhile. As well as making some money for LCGC (and being able to purchase more and better equipment), they added to the choir's reputation by establishing themselves as efficient, hard-working, knowledgeable and reliable. What more could any client ask?

Another way in which we raised the money to support our activities was by having a dedicated sales team, who arranged the production of sweatshirts, tee-shirts, badges, stickers, tapes and records, and sold them enthusiastically to our supporters at concerts.

In the early years of the choir's life Andrea acted as our Press and Publicity Officer while she was at home with the babies. Gradually this became a bigger and bigger job, with demand for photographs, promotional packs, subscriptions to the mailing list (no email in those days – just stamps on envelopes and trips to the post office!), interviews and of course *On the Rock*. She helped organize sponsors who subsidized our uniforms and even the minibus.

We also had a promotions department (Howard Francis, Claudette Brown and Lawrence Johnson) who organized the tours – an immensely complex job – and booked and managed studio sessions and agency work for other groups, choirs, soloists and musicians. They also handled the organizing and teaching of Gospel music workshops, which became an increasingly important part of our life. Often an LCGC team would visit a city for a week at a time, working with children and young people and leading Gospel music workshops and seminars within schools, churches and youth and community organizations.

By 1998 we had amassed a great deal of experience. At that point Andrea was contacted by the African Caribbean Evangelical Alliance, who had been asked by the Millennium Commission to organize events to enable the churches to celebrate 2,000 years of the Christian faith. There was a call for bids, so Andrea got together with Juliet Fletcher, another pioneer in Gospel music. She and Andrea were good friends and had a great track record in dreaming up ideas for us to put into practice! Their concept was to put on a Millennium Festival of Gospel – G2K – which would embrace the whole Gospel music industry, but first they needed us to be the lead organization. They brought together LCGC and the African Caribbean Evangelical Alliance in a partnership to promote and develop Gospel music and arts in Britain and Europe. This was the origin of the British Gospel Arts Consortium.

Apparently there were limits on the use of the term "British" in such a title, and for formal incorporation the organization had to provide documentation to support their claim to use it. Andrea arranged for the British Council to send a letter confirming that they used LCGC in Africa to represent Britain and British Gospel music. That did the trick and we were allowed to use the name. As Andrea wrote in the festival programme:

"J" (formerly known as Juliet), Bazil and I have been planning and praying for such a platform for Gospel music for the last twenty-plus years. Well, this festival is the first of many to come. Gospel will take its rightful place in our communities, schools, music venues and airwaves… as we spread light and shake salt to brighten and give good taste to a despairing world.

Alongside the main festival she hoped to have a schools' programme, and again she planned for something tremendous. She wanted to research what was happening in schools all over the country, and establish how much Gospel music education went on. It would have been a huge undertaking to set up the system she initially dreamed of (an umbrella body for Gospel music education all over the country, so that common standards and policies were established) but it would have been wonderful. What she found was that apart from London, there was not much activity anywhere except for a few artists in Nottingham, Manchester and Birmingham. British Gospel Arts organized workshops in a number of schools across England, ending with the opportunity to come and perform at the National Festival for School Gospel Choirs, part of the G2K Festival in May 2000 at the Shepherds Bush Empire, London.

The schools festival featured a guest children's choir from Barnardo's in Redbridge, and also William Morris School, Waltham Forest, where the children had learning disabilities. This evidence of inclusion (which was very important to Andrea) had a huge impact. The LCGC tutors had never taught people with disabilities before, and they were shocked when they first visited William Morris to conduct the workshops. However, they succeeded in transforming the students into a real Gospel choir, and it was amazing to see them taking a full part in events alongside the other schools.

Interestingly, in 2009 we visited William Morris School again, and found their choir still going strong and producing their third CD. Touchingly, in one corridor there was a noticeboard that was in effect a shrine to British Gospel Arts, with photographs, programmes and their certificates from the festival. It had meant so much to the staff that British Gospel Arts believed in their children; they too recognized the potential that was there and decided to continue the Gospel choir.

For G2K we also had a Gala Celebration of Gospel Choirs over two evenings, and gathered together newly established and well-known choirs. They included the Stavanger Gospel Choir from Norway and Hands of Praise from Jamaica, as well as choirs from all over the UK. Some sang traditional spirituals, others rhythm and blues, and some sang in the mother tongues of Africa. The G2K Workshop Choir (drawn from guest choirs) featured guest musicians Chris Brown, Joshua McKenzie, Adrian McKenzie and Floyd Millen.

Diversity was important: Peter Daley, who was studying composition at the Birmingham Conservatoire, wrote some original works which were premiered at the festival. Andrea, who came from Trinidad and Tobago, had always wanted to fuse Gospel with Indian music. Peter Daley's new works for Gospel song and sitar did just that. She engaged Asif Bhatti, a Pakistani Christian singer and musician who played tabla, sitar and harmonium. He and his fellow musicians joined in the venture which mixed the sounds of Asia with Gospel. All the evening performances were signed by BASLIN (the Black and Asian Sign Language Interpreters' Network), which was another first for a Gospel music event.

British Gospel Arts continues to grow, a thriving arts organization working in schools and communities across London and running workshops as far afield as Ireland, Scotland and Italy. It is the education arm of LCGC, and its aim is to promote and develop Gospel music in Britain and Europe through education, employment, performance and research. It runs courses for individuals and groups, both adults and children, including people with learning difficulties, helping them to find or articulate their voice, learn new rhythms and sing as a group. It also operates workshops focused on using music and performing arts to influence the lifestyle of young people, promoting citizenship, good mental health and positive life choices.

Andrea is the Arts Director of BGA, and she has gathered a powerful team of leaders and tutors: myself as Principal, Cecil Chambers, Viv Broughton and Karen Gibson as Directors, and our daughter Vernetta Lynch as Project Manager for Schools.

Their latest big venture is The Sing Thing, which is part of a

London Sing Up Community partnership project with ARK Music, iGospel and Newham's Young People Chorus. The Sing Thing works with children and young people from seven to nineteen years old in North and East London, running five singing clubs, three in schools and two open to everyone; parents are encouraged to come and sing with their children. They are immensely popular and the regular concerts are always packed with enthusiastic audiences.

It's good to know that there is another generation coming up that is filled with enthusiasm for Gospel music, and which feels itself a part of LCGC.

The choir itself is still involved in charitable work of all kinds. Not long ago I was contacted by a man named Ian Hamilton. He is the CEO of Compassion International, a charity whose motto is "Releasing children from poverty in Jesus' name". He invited me to join him on a trip to Uganda to launch a new spin-off charity called Fountain of Peace. Peace is a young lady from Kyonjojo who herself benefited from sponsorship by a British member of Compassion International. This enabled her to complete her education and go to university. She is now married with children, and has returned to her home area to join in the fight against poverty.

When I arrived at Kyonjojo village I was shocked by the conditions: there was no clean water available, and people were drinking and washing in a stream contaminated with animal effluent. There was no medical help for miles. It was such a contrast to our comfortable lives in the UK, and yet the people all seemed to be happy and smiling, and the children all looked beautiful and clean, in spite of the lack of proper food and water.

We decided that the most urgent priority was a supply of clean water, which meant digging wells. Other plans included purchasing land to build homes, a school and a clinic, and paying for doctors to visit regularly. As soon as we came home we organized a concert in a church in Woodford Green, in Essex, to launch our appeal. The choir were enthusiastic about adopting Fountain of Peace as one of "our" charities, and we got the appeal off to a good start. The land has been purchased and work has begun on building the new houses, and we have continued to have a strong connection with Kyonjojo and its people ever since.

It's clear to me that LCGC will never be "just" a choir – our Christian faith leads us in too many other directions, as we try to live out our faith in practical ways and show Jesus' love in everything we do. That's an aim and an ambition to which, in the words of the song, "My soul says yes".

CHAPTER **10**

We've come a mighty long way

When LCGC started life in 1983, the idea that we could ever be full-time musicians was just a distant dream. We didn't even expect to get singing engagements that would pay us. We were members, in effect, of a glorified musical youth club, eighty to a hundred young people who were having fun, enjoying our music, and trying to learn more and improve our technique while praising our God. We rejoiced in the opportunity to share our faith: in those days it was really exciting to receive an invitation to perform from a non-church organization – now we perform more often outside churches than within them.

The administrative set-up was very different, too: then our office consisted of a desk, phone and filing cabinet in the bedroom; now we employ eight or so full-time workers to manage the operation.

The membership of the choir has changed, as well. In the early 1980s our members were drawn from the Caribbean-led Pentecostal churches, and people in those days lived out their faith in a different way. There were strict dress codes and limits on acceptable out-of-church activities; there were fewer distractions for Christian young people. The choir offered them not just music but new friends, travel and excitement, and also an opportunity to live out their faith. Our members were fervent in their desire to share the Gospel; their heartfelt dedication and commitment was evident.

Our members are still all Christians, but they don't share a common church background as we did then. Now about 50 per cent of our members are of African origin (mainly Nigerians and Ugandans), who have been born in the UK or who have moved here with their parents at an early age, so they have been educated here. On the last audition lists I saw only two or three Caribbean names.

In those early days the Gospel community was not catered for in the entertainment industry in any fashion – now things are very different. Our music gets exposure on TV, radio and live events; there are full-time Gospel singers and musicians; and if our young people are ambitious to become solo stars, they have a real chance of making a name for themselves.

One thing which hasn't changed, however, is the centrality of the Gospel message. At festivals and concerts the only apparent difference between us and the rock bands is that we may have twenty or thirty people on stage at once. Our attitude to delivering a professional performance is the same: the audience has come to be entertained. But there is something more: we also know that they will hear the message of faith in God contained in our music. That is the one outstanding thing that all our choir members mention: the pleasure they get from singing to a non-church audience, seeing them visibly moved by our words and sharing our joy. That's a greater blessing to us than preaching to the converted, or singing inside the church community.

LCGC has been my life for the last twenty-eight years, and it has been my family's life too. The children are all grown up now.

Vernetta is a great singer and a great mum; she and her husband Sam Lynch have three children, Jenniah-Mae, Jonel and Brianna. Sam is a bass player, writer and producer, and together with his sisters Ruth and Tula and Vernetta's cousin Semele, he and Vernetta started a band called V9, singing funk/soul with Gospel lyrics.

Their album *World to Me*[24] was released in 2010. Vernetta conducted LCGC for a time; she's also a talented make-up artist and the Administrator for British Gospel Arts, working with her mum.

Leonn is the drummer for LCGC and other bands, and he writes and produces songs. He has also given us three lovely grandchildren, baby Kiki and the twins Micah and Hayden.

Stephanie is a professional singer – she used to conduct the choir and sometimes still sings with us. She is also a songwriter and is recording her own album with her husband, Ayo Oyerinde, a keyboard musician. Together they run their own production company, T'ayce of Pie, and they are vocal arrangers, writers and producers for several songs on LCGC albums. They have one son, Asa.

My first son, Marlon, is the only one who doesn't work in music (though he plays keyboard in church). We were very close when he was young, but unfortunately I had to take a smaller role in his life during his teenage years when I married and was less able to spend time with him. He worked for a firm in the City for a while, but was introduced to drugs, and eventually lost his job. I see him regularly and I try to support him as best I can. We have a good relationship, though he knows I am frustrated at the waste of so much potential.

My last child, Ce'anna, is a beautiful and precious little girl. Born in a later phase of my life, she is already showing promise in her musical abilities.

Sadly, over the years Andrea and I drifted apart, and in 2006 we agreed to divorce. However, we still work together, and Andrea plays a key role in the life of the choir in her leadership of British Gospel Arts. She supported me and the choir from its conception, and her inventive ideas for new avenues for LCGC to explore, and her sheer hard work in developing and establishing them, mean that a great deal of the choir's unique nature has Andrea's energy and imagination at its heart.

The choir began to diversify almost immediately it was formed: for instance, the prison ministry was a practical outworking of our faith which developed in our first year, but other elements soon followed. We soon realized that we could not rely entirely on volunteer labour – we needed to pay our musical directors and later some administrative staff to handle bookings and so on. Finding the money for paid staff led us to focus on our financial stewardship. When we bought amplifying equipment and sound systems we hired them out to other groups when we weren't using them ourselves, maximizing the return for our investment. We realized that our skills and expertise were also marketable, so we offered workshops and general advice. This was how the London Gospel Centre began: it was planned to be the place where all things "Gospel" happened – teaching, advice, rehearsal, equipment hire, artist bookings and a café.

That arrangement has evolved over the years into a much more complex organization. The education work, whether for individuals, groups or schools, comes under the umbrella of British Gospel Arts. The administration of the choir is handled by Choir Connexion, the management arm of LCGC. The staff may be dealing with bookings for several events at the same time – for instance, a couple of weddings (with different costume requirements and travel arrangements, as well as selecting available performers) while a larger group is on tour (flights, baggage, ticketing, accommodation, foreign agents, timings for sound checks and performances and a million other little points). Choir Connexion is the point of contact for anyone wanting to make an LCGC booking, and the team is wonderful at making sure everything runs smoothly.

We also run REV – The Session Agency ("REV" stands for Real Entertainment Value, but it's also the choir's nickname for me). The agency assists clients in putting together an evening's entertainment, handling corporate, promotional and private events and supplying singers, function bands, string quartets and even orchestras. The pool of artists they draw on is not limited to (but may include) LCGC singers – we have agency singers who are not choir members. REV uses the expertise we have developed over the years in organizing events, and operates this as a business which supplies work for "our" singers and others. This was one of our original priorities – to enable Gospel musicians to realize their ambitions to become professionals and make their living from music.

MVLS is our own record label and publishing company (the name is made up of the children's initials: Marlon, Vernetta, Leonn and Stephanie). We set it up to enable us to take control of an important aspect of our activities – recording. Our latest venture is setting up Brookdale Studios, our own recording facility. This had been a part of my vision for many years, and when we moved into Brookdale House (where the LCGC offices are now housed) I put in several applications for funding to help us turn the building into a recording studio. An architect drew up the plans and we contacted everyone from the Mayor's Office in London (with whom we had many meetings) to the Arts Council. Andrea put together a brilliant proposal for using the studio to help local children develop their musical skills, but it all came to nothing. The Arts Council said, "This is a fantastic organisation with many great achievements, providing great role models, doing wonderful community work, and well spoken of in the media" – but no money was forthcoming.

At the end of 2009 I was reflecting on the achievement of so many of my dreams. REV – The Session Agency was doing well and the record label was up and running, but downstairs in Brookdale House was still referred to by the staff as "The Dungeon", used mostly as a store for instruments, with a few bits of recording equipment in one room. I looked at my age (nearing 60) and decided I couldn't leave it any longer. I wasn't willing to go round with the begging bowl any more. I was going to have to make it happen myself.

I met a builder and invited him to look at the premises. He had never built a recording studio before, but he was willing to try, and in January 2010 he brought in a skip and started knocking walls down. It was slightly alarming: I had only the haziest idea of the budget and no idea where the money was going to come from. I talked to my financial adviser, dug into my pension plan and hoped for the best. I have always been a person who is willing to take a risk, but I feel happier if I can take the risk on my own head. I wanted to go ahead on the strength of that gut feeling that this was the moment to do it, and I didn't want to consult or negotiate with funding bodies. I had such a strong feeling that this was the right thing to do right now.

At the time of writing (August 2010) the studio is already in use. It isn't completed yet (I'm still spending) but already I feel that its success is assured. It has brought a wonderful new energy into the organization, because we know we can make our own decisions about what and when we record. It is also available for hire, there are plenty of enquiries coming in, and we hope it will pay its way in its first year. The other great advantage is that the family (all of whom are recording artists) don't have to go looking for studios when they want to record their own material – we have one on the premises.

There's no doubt that we have come "a mighty long way" from those early days, when we thought we were bringing some young people together for just one concert! What does the future hold for LCGC? I don't know, of course – it's in God's hands. I don't know who will take over the helm when I finally retire (though the choir and team tell me that I shouldn't say the R-word). I'm hoping that person will appear, and that I'll recognize them when they come along. We will go on working as hard as ever, but I keep telling our staff and members to try to find time to enjoy our success. I suppose I would like to have life move at a slightly more leisurely pace; for instance, recording an album, spending a couple of years promoting it, then taking time out to write more and make another recording. That would be a good cycle of work.

At the moment we work all year round. The studio, the session agency and the LCGC brand are all busy and functioning efficiently, and all constantly generating more work. This is a good thing – I feel very strongly the responsibility of employing people. They all have families and mortgages, and I need to be a good businessman in order to generate the income to pay them all.

LCGC tries to keep a balance between business and faith. I'm aware that there are artists who earn more than we do – and between the choir members and the team we have a lot more mouths to feed than a four-piece band. I have a responsibility to maximize our earning potential, which means some effective negotiating when it comes to bookings. I delegate that responsibility to people who have the heart for it. I appreciate their skills, but I remind everyone that our work is more than just playing, singing, negotiating or doing the administration. Everyone needs to own the dream and do their work with passion. That's why I won't employ people who are just looking for a career in the music industry – they are always in transit. I want people who care about Gospel music and whose faith is alive in their hearts. They can share our vision and become part of the LCGC family.

Even though the choir members no longer share the same church background, and we have changed from a "gathered" church choir to a success in the entertainment business, faith is still at the centre. We don't ever go on stage without a time of devotion and prayer. When we travel, everyone takes a turn at leading devotions on the bus and at the venue – and occasionally after the concert, too.

During a concert I often link the songs by talking a little about them; I may feel led to talk about the content of a song, develop the idea and bring the lyrics alive a little. For instance, sometimes we sing "My Change Will Come": "If I can hold out, if I can keep the faith, in God's own time, my change will come." I talk about how we hope for and desire something, but sometimes we're disappointed. Relationships break down, jobs are lost, and we sit at home waiting for the phone to ring. We lose faith in ourselves, or blame God for things that happen because of our own actions. But if we put our trust in God, he'll show us the way back to the light.

There's no point in preaching a sermon – it's not the time or place for it – but I try to explain the Gospel songs in terms that relate to people's own lives. Then when we sing the song they may begin to have some understanding of the hope of the Gospel, and the power of faith.

I feel that I've been so privileged to have been given the talent and the opportunity to play and sing Gospel music. It's something I'd like all our musicians to recognize: what our fingers and our voices do is only an extension of God's touch in the deepest part of who we are. It's a gift we can use to communicate with other people, and every day I thank God for that. We can use our hands and voices not only to please the ear but also to reach the spirit. I feel blessed because I believe in my heart that I received my gift from God. Every day I pray and meditate on what he has done, and ask for his inspiration and guidance.

I believe that as Gospel artists we have a responsibility not just to talk or sing about our faith in God; we should also try to enlighten others about the benefits of having a personal relationship with him. When our lives connect with God, then we view all our activities – our life's work, our families, leisure, nature, everything we do on a daily basis – with a deeper appreciation. God has created us and given us life, and that gift of new life, our faith in our Lord Jesus Christ, is a blessing to us as individuals. We must pass it on so it can be a blessing to others too.

Notes

1. A person from Barbados

2. Peter Rachman (1919–1962) was a landlord in London who owned many slum properties. He became notorious for driving out sitting tenants who were protected by rent controls, in order to re-let properties to new tenants (mainly immigrants) at much higher rents.

3. "When the morning comes" by Charles A. Tindley

4. The Latter Rain movement had started after the Second World War, amid the Evangelical/Pentecostal revival led by preachers like Billy Graham and Oral Roberts. The "former rain" referred to Pentecost, the first outpouring of the Holy Spirit on the disciples of Jesus; the "latter rain" was the blessing seen in the new churches springing up at this time.

5. Luke 15:11–32

6. Exodus 7:16

7. "Jim Crow" was an abusive expression used to describe African Americans in the early twentieth century. Legislation was passed in various states which prevented black people from voting or holding public office, and enforced segregation in public places, transport, schools, restaurants and facilities like public toilets and drinking fountains.

8. Paul Robeson was a bass-baritone singer and actor.

9. "I shall not be moved" was originally a spiritual which was changed (in the same way as "I'll overcome") to a collective voice ("We shall not be moved") for use in protest.

10. Now the Bishop of Ruach Ministries.

11. A talent show which ran on ITV from 1956 to 1978.

12. Simon Heaven (1947–2007) ran Compass Films, which made many documentaries for Channel 4 and the BBC. Many of Simon's films and photographs focused on social injustice.

13. Trevor Phillips worked in television as a researcher and presenter before becoming Head of Current Affairs for London Weekend Television. He is now Chair of the Equality and Human Rights Commission.

14. Released in 1983 by Stiff Records.

15. Released in May 1970 by Apple Records.

16. A breakfast television programme which ran on ITV from 1983 to 1992.

17. Gordon Lorenz (1949–2011) worked with many world-famous artists and produced over 800 recordings during his career.

18. Released in 2004 by Mercury Records.

19. Will Young's debut album released in October 2002 by 19 Recordings, RCA, BMG.

20. Released in February 1999 by Food Records, EMI.

21. Released in October 1995 by Mute Records and Elektra Records.

22. Released in September 2004 by Mute Records.

23. Released in May 2005 by Parlophone Records.

24. Released independently by V9 Collective.

Discography

Feel the Spirit

Format: Album – Vinyl, Cassette
Label: Myrrh
Year: 1986

1 – How I Got Over

2 – I Really Feel the Spirit

3 – He Walks Beside Me

4 – Perfect Harmony

5 – Pass Me Not

6 – Joy of the Lord

7 – My Soul Says Yes

8 – All to Jesus

9 – Oh Happy Day

10 – Coming Again So Soon

Gospel Greats

Format: Album – CD, Cassette
Label: EMI
Year: 1990

1 – Swing Low Sweet Chariot

2 – Precious Lord

3 – Amazing Grace

4 – Nobody Knows the Trouble I've Seen

5 – What a Friend We Have In Jesus

6 – Kumbayah

7 – Count Your Blessings

8 – Love Lifted Me

9 – When the Saints Go Marching In

10 – There is a Green Hill Far Away

11 – Oh Happy Day

12 – The Old Rugged Cross

Hush and Listen

Format: Album – CD, Cassette
Label: Kingsway
Year: 1993

1 – The Root

2 – Somebody's Calling My Name

3 – I'll Take You There

4 – Knockin' on Heaven's Door

5 – Let Me Have it All

6 – In Your Hands

7 – Ball of Confusion

8 – One Man

9 – Respect Yourself

10 – Sans Souci

11 – Learning to Love

12 – You Can Make it

13 – Nobody Knows

14 – Abraham, Martin & John

15 – Oh Happy Day

16 – Coming Together

Live! Inspiration and Power

Format: Album – CD, Cassette
Label: MVLS Records
Year: 1996

1 – Praise the Lord

2 – Great is the Lord

3 – Holy, Holy, Holy

4 – Oh Happy Day

5 – Fill My Cup

6 – Bridge Over Troubled Water

7 – Cast Your Burdens

8 – I Really Feel the Spirit

9 – So Strong

10 – Constant Love

Out of Many, One Voice

Format: Album – CD, Cassette
Label: FAR
Year: 1998

1 – Happy are the People

2 – Found Myself a Reason

3 – Every Passing Minute

4 – He is Worthy

5 – It's Not Magic

6 – Back in the Fold

7 – Call on Him

8 – Interlude

9 – Feel the Spirit

10 – Teach Me Oh Lord

11 – Stand Up

Negro Spirituals and Gospel Songs

Format: Album – CD, Cassette
Label: MVLS Records
Year: 1999

1 – Welcome

2 – I Go to the Rock

3 – If I Can Hold Out

4 – Let Me Live My Life

5 – Amen/This Little Light of Mine

6 – Kumbayah

7 – Bread of Heaven

8 – Jesus is Alive

9 – It's Not Magic

10 – Holy, Holy

11 – Glory to the Son

12 – Oh When the Saints

13 – Oh Happy Day

Joy to the World

Format: Album – CD, Cassette
Label: FAR
Year: 1999

1 – This is the Reason

2 – Holy Night

3 – How I Love to be with You

4 – Joy to the World

5 – Silent Night

6 – Just be Love

7 – Angels from the Realms of Glory

8 – Christmas Medley: When was Jesus

Born/Go Tell it on the Mountain/Glory

Hallelujah

9 – Come, O Come Emmanuel

Fill My Cup

Format: Single – Vinyl
Label: Universal/Island records
Year: 1999

1 – Fill My Cup

Force Behind the Power

Format: Album – CD, Cassette
Label: MVLS Records
Year: 2001

1 – *Instead of Begging*

2 – *The Force Behind the Power*

3 – *Faith*

4 – *Whenever You Call*

5 – *I Will Wait*

6 – *He Loves Me Lots*

7 – *Where Could I Go?*

8 – *If I Can Hold Out*

9 – *Never Alone*

10 – *I've Found the Answer*

11 – *Tell Me What's Going on*

21st Anniversary Concert, Live at Abbey Road

Format: Album – CD, DVD, Video, Cassette
Label: Kingsway Music
Year: 2003

1 – *How I Got Over*

2 – *Faith*

3 – *The Living Years*

4 – *Back in the Fold*

5 – *My Soul Says Yes*

6 – *Blessed Be Your Name (feat. Matt Redman)*

7 – *I Could Sing of Your Love Forever*

8 – *Some Day*

9 – *In the Garden (feat. Sam Moore)*

10 – *I Surrender All (feat. Carleen Anderson)*

11 – *Dance*

12 – *Our Song*

Keep Moving

Format: Album – CD
Label: MVLS Records
Year: 2007

1 – Intro

2 – The Answer

3 – I Need Your Spirit

4 – Found Myself a Reason

5 – Difference In Me

6 – Dance

7 – Ark

8 – Born Again

9 – He Loves Me Lots

10 – Magic

11 – Praise Worthy

12 – Never Alone

13 – Keep Moving

14 – God is Love

Glorious

Format: Album – CD
Label: BMG
Year: 2010

1 – One

2 – Hallelujah

3 – When the Saints Go Marching In

4 – Soul to Soul – (Guest vocals Paul Carrack)

5 – Let it be

6 – Glory, Glory, Hallelujah

7 – Down In the River to Pray

8 – Now That We Found Love

9 – Amazing Grace

10 – Abide with Me

11 – Swing Low…

12 – We Shall Overcome

13 – God is Love